'Wallace and Mary's refreshingly honest book about the joys and struggles of serving God in an historic denomination will bring huge encouragement to many. Time and again we read of the poor and disadvantaged finding faith, often in spite of the church's limitations. This is a call to persevere and a story of hope.'

Nick Cuthbert

'There is here that most powerful of Christian combinations: the sharing of experience and the ability to learn – and therefore teach – from it. Many mountains of despair and complacency will be moved by this book.'

Peter Selby, Bishop of Worcester

'What is a clergyman to do when the church's institutional ways prove an obstacle to gospel living? Wallace and Mary Brown have lived this question for many years. In this homely, earthy and honest book it is the impoverished, marginalised, rejected and apparently hopeless who show them what church is being called to become. This book raises fundamental questions for all churches and the questions, when faced, bring hope.'

Gerard W. Hughes, author of The God of Surprises

To our friends Martin and Janet Knox,
who have always worked alongside us
on the adventure of faith.

Walking on the Moon

Wallace and Mary Brown

First published 2004

Names have been changed except when accompanied by a surname. Personal information has often been composited to offer complete anonymity.

ISBN 1 84291 181 3

NexGen is an imprint of
KINGSWAY COMMUNICATIONS LTD
Lottbridge Drove, Eastbourne BN23 6NT, England.
Email: books@kingsway.co.uk

Book design and production for the publishers by
Bookprint Creative Services, P.O. Box 827, BN21 3YJ, England.
Printed in Great Britain.

Contents

Preface

> 'Let my people go, so that they may worship me . . .' With a mighty hand the Lord brought us out of Egypt, out of the land of slavery. (Exodus 8:1 and 13:14)

Nearly two decades ago, God placed his amazing 'angels on the walls' of our church/vicarage complex. For Mary and me it was the start of a wonderful yet painful spiritual journey of discovering God's heart for the poor and needy and beyond.

As we have travelled and spoken nationwide, we've met many devout, faithful Christians who clearly love the Lord. Our angels story has met with an anointing wherever it has been told, and we witness that people are clamouring for God's spiritual power to reign supreme in their fellowships. The intrinsic joys and longings of faith are there for all to see.

Yet there is also a profound frustration. Revival has not come, despite many proclamations and much prayer. The British church is not growing, regardless of stories of wonderful moves of the Spirit throughout our global village. The general populace appears totally removed from true church life, yet still caught up to some extent with 'folk religion', and the media delight to portray Christians as narrow-minded, bigoted, 'religious' people who have little to say about life or spirituality.

Jesus himself, during his earthly life, saw institutionalised, legalistic religion as the major obstacle to true faith; the practices that 'shut the kingdom of heaven in men's faces' (Matthew 23:13). Today, the church ensconces few of the religious trappings of the scribes and Pharisees of old. Yet society so often perceives 'church' as a barrier rather than an open door into God's holy presence; an institution whose sole purpose is to maintain historic buildings and lead 'folk' festivals.

At the same time, devout Christians long to see God's church as a wholly vibrant, faith-filled, living expression of the 'body of Christ', yet are exasperated by a system which tends to exclude dynamic faith and hold congregations in bondage to a status quo. Also many church leaders are caught up in this system, which in my experience causes vibrant faith to be lost, vocation to be questioned and a hidden apathy to emerge.

I want to take us on a journey. God demands, as Moses did of Pharaoh all those years ago, 'Let my people go, so that they may worship me.' This book expresses a longing for God's church to be released from its barren moonscape of slavery to imprisoning systems, which makes faith inaccessible to many. It calls for the church herself to reconsider the presentation of her unchangeable gospel so that biblical truth can be taught and modelled to our increasingly uninformed postmodern generation. It proposes that unhelpful barriers, in all Christian streams, be removed through the faith dynamic of the Jesus way so that we may be able to say again, with Moses, 'with a mighty hand the Lord brought us out of Egypt, out of the land of slavery'.

In this book I hope to lead towards a 'Jesus-centred

church'. A church holding tight to the Scriptures, and to the Spirit's teaching over the centuries. A church rejoicing in the breadth of old and new Christian streams while retaining precious truth from the past. A church that repentantly rejects religion for religion's sake and seeks to make the church institution the servant of the gospel, rather than the master. A church where 'folk religion' is exposed while ensuring that spiritual comfort is available to all. A church that is continually and radically pursuing the Spirit of God to take all that is barren and make it fertile.

My prayer is that *Walking on the Moon* will challenge us to develop a vibrant church on fire for God, which continually re-shapes herself to impact the people of the twenty-first century. A church that presents the gospel in an accessible way, thereby continuing to be the Holy Spirit's co-worker drawing men, women and children to a saving knowledge of the Lord Jesus Christ.

Introduction

> He lifted me out of the slimy pit, out of the mud and mire; he set my feet on a rock and gave me a firm place to stand. (Psalm 40:2)

The paint-peeled steel door swung shut with a dull clunk as Gaynor shouted coarsely at the officer, 'F*** you too, mate,' and stuck up one finger in an equally obscene gesture. She closed her eyes in anger as she stood there and then, as if overcome, her shapely young body collapsed down onto the cell bench, and her head struck the dirty grey tiles sharply. But the resulting pain was nothing compared with the ache of her body and its need for another fix.

As the hours crawled by she paced the nine by nine room before sitting screwed up in the toilet corner. She would have done *anything* for even one Methadone tablet, let alone the cool white powder. But the prison held Gaynor as nothing else had ever done in her stained life.

The officer rattled the door. 'Cuppa tea, love?' he said with a note of care.

Gaynor raised her eyes sullenly. 'For God's sake! What would I do with yer bloody tea, you . . .'

Yet strangely that simple act of human compassion touched her. It drew her turmoiled, tortured mind back to her Sunday school days. With a sudden and amazing clarity the meaning of that long-forgotten childhood faith spoke into her ravaged body and soul. She began to feel and to think beyond the heroin. And then, wondrously and supernaturally, Jesus was there with her in what had been a bleak, desolate, pain-filled cell. Gaynor was totally caught up with a presence of absolute purity and love, cocooning her in warmth and light, which completely marginalised all the horror of 'cold turkey' and, even more importantly, rent the hardness of her glacial heart.

A few months later Gaynor sobbed her story to a couple of Christian listeners at the back of St Boniface Church. 'God came to me. I know it was Jesus. He spoke to me. It was as if I was lying in his arms, with my whole self mapped out before him. Oh! I can't explain it any better. I just knew it was God, see?' She lifted her tear-stained eyes with a questioning look. What would these 'religious' people make of her? Would they too simply condemn her?

They didn't really say anything, but she felt it was OK, and she decided that she could continue.

'It wasn't so bad after that – you know, coming off the "stuff". But it's been the guilt that's really hit me. The children. I've got a whole brood, you know. What have I done to them?'

As vicar of this council estate church, I didn't manage to talk to Gaynor for some time. I was an authority figure, an untouchable, a dog collar that she shrank away from. Yet the Christ-meeting in the prison cell had driven her to the local church on her release. She would slink in at the back – every Sunday and other days too.

Viv, one of the intercessors who took Gaynor to heart, said to me quietly, 'You know, Wallace, I was thinking. If all we had to offer was just "churchy religion", it would have been hopeless for Gaynor. It would have ravaged that lovely experience – the sheer reality of meeting Jesus in the prison cell that brought her here.' Viv paused thoughtfully for a moment and then went on, 'She even said to me, "If it had been all that usual church crap, there's no way I'd have stayed here for a moment."' Viv took out a tissue. 'She just wanted to meet Jesus again. And she has!' She blew her nose with gusto – to stop the tears, I think.

This book is dedicated to Gaynor. And to all the Gaynors of our broken, flawed society today. It is dedicated to all who wish to push aside the cobwebs of unwelcoming 'religion' and the system of our institutionalised, often clique-dominated church, and meet with the living Lord. It is dedicated to those who pray that faith will dictate the way we should be church in the twenty-first century so that we can reap the gold of the past and yet at the same time be open to the Spirit for the future. It is dedicated to those who do not want to 'dumb down' into a postmodern 'anything goes' sort of spirituality, yet who want to reach people for whom 'religion' has become an anachronistic obstacle to faith: a reason not to search for God. It is dedicated to all who want to see God at work in our society, transforming it from the inside out so that men, women and children can be saved.

It is also dedicated to the suffering and pain of Christians like Gaynor, who struggled and still struggle to be a Christian in an alien world. The past still has power, and the present – rather than a light-filled walk of joy – is a battle against self, circumstances and Satan. I often speak about the wonderful power of the Saviour and then fall headlong into a dark place of self-doubt and God-doubt and cynicism. That's how it is.

Faith in Christ calls us to throw ourselves, warts and all, at the feet of Jesus Christ and admit that we are sinners in need of a Saviour. Faith is an adventure that must take us beyond any human institution into a world where even the Son of Man himself suffered the humiliating torture of being nailed to a cross shouting, 'My God, my God, why have you forsaken me?' as he took the sins of the world upon himself.

Finally, this book is dedicated to those who want God's people to take the lid off systemised religion so that church can be a pro-active word, telling of a pilgrim people reaching out to God. And finding him. Not merely assuaging human need for religious ritual and rite, but being caught up in his supernatural presence and power.

I start this journey from the inside – from inside the institution where God has called me to be a vicar, and from thence a 'canon' . . .

1

'Stuff'

> . . . to prepare God's people for works of service, so that the body of Christ may be built up. (Ephesians 4:12)

The verger glided silently before me. He was dressed in full regalia, with a 'wand' tucked under his arm and that certain supercilious expression of the religious rite 'expert'. Up to the large oak door at the rear of Birmingham Cathedral he flowed as I panted behind carrying a small suitcase containing borrowed cassock, much repaired surplice and my brand new canon's scarf. Mary, wearing the new outfit we had argued over in Marks & Spencer's, was intently sorting out a front pew for herself and our children.

What a mixture of emotions. Here was I, supposedly a profound advocate of transforming the church to meet the people and culture of today, being swallowed up by the system and being ushered into the cathedral bowels ready for a traditional robed choir, chanted psalms and a stiffly formal edition of sung evensong at which I was to be made a canon of the Church of England. The picture was completed by a time-warp bewigged lawyer pushing an ancient, embossed red leather bound book in front of me. 'Where's the quill pen?' I would have quipped if I hadn't felt so out of my depth.

Yet it was also so brilliant! As I processed alongside other would-be canons with the archdeacons and bishops, I saw my three children standing next to Mary. They looked proud and pleased, and my heart swelled. Jeremy, Nicholas and Elizabeth had more than merely survived the terror epoch of the Quinton Mob, Crazy Carl hurling building bricks at the vicarage window, and all the other social nightmares of a deprived neighbourhood.[1] So many people have asked us, over the years, 'But what about your children? Is it fair on them to live in such an area?' Yet here they were, all committed Christians, having travelled many miles to be alongside their mum and dad on this occasion. Alongside us in body, mind and spirit! What more could a father ask? God is so good and so faithful.

The bishop stood in full regalia to read the Canon's Charge, ending with the archdeacon leading me by the hand into the deep oaken recesses of the choir end of the cathedral to my 'stall'. Led away from Mary and my family and even, perhaps, from reality, into a dark entanglement of an ecclesiastical ego trip within the religious system.

As the service progressed, my mind wandered back to the early days in our outer council estate parish when I arrived as a rookie vicar. I remembered being stunned that a pathetically young looking mother of five had sat in a corner and simply watched her husband commit suicide, cutting open both wrists. Why hadn't she fetched help? Of course, I knew nothing about domestic violence and disempowerment in those early days. All I knew was that she sat, head and body bowed, surrounded by her maltreated children as the blood seeped out, just a few short feet away, for four long hours.

And what about the double murder a few weeks after our

---

[1] Wallace and Mary Brown, *Angels on the Walls* (Kingsway, 2000).

family arrived? How was the family of that tragic social worker coping these years later? What about the four children? After all, they had seen their own mother murdered, along with the woman trying to help her, and their convicted father was serving life – or was he out now, trying to see them?

And then there was the child who had been tied to a lamp post and burned with cigarette ends. Did his body and mind still bear the scars?

The congregation wearily stood as the organ struck up for yet another hymn and I realised I'd missed the sermon.

And what about the infamous Quinton Mob that had been so firmly routed by our 'angels on the walls'? I'd met quite a few ex-members from time to time and even shared the story. One was now an ex-SAS soldier; he looked rather pleased and quite touched by the account. He'd told me he'd become a Christian. What about all the others? Did the angels somehow touch their souls as well?

Our account of the Quinton Angels has travelled all over the world. Surprisingly, the story of God's angelic presence has never been scorned, but the anointing has risen mostly out of the pain that Mary and I suffered as we sought to follow the Lord. And from the power of estate people telling their personal stories.

Take a church in the midst of a troubled Northern Ireland estate where Mary and I, together with four of our folk, led a mission weekend. Near to that church, a huge painting of a balaclava-clad gunman looked down from a prominent gable end. 'The other week, a young man blew himself up under that mural,' shared a pained resident called Celia. 'Can you imagine what was going on in his mind to do that? It's like this whole area is held in bondage to that horrible picture. It just dominates the estate with evil.' I could see the tears in Celia's eyes and I noticed that Gaynor was already putting her arms around her. It was as if she understood from the inside. Not about gunmen perhaps, but certainly about the evil hold on people's lives, because of her violent and drug abused past. How amazing that Gaynor had survived the prison cell to become a sort of missionary – even though she was far from sorted herself.

Celia went on: 'It's like you were saying about your Quinton Mob before the angels. Like God has just deserted the place. And here we are doing our religious services not more than a few hundred yards from that wicked mural. Surely we should be doing *something!*' Her voice rose with the pain of the situation and the seeming powerlessness of the church. 'But what on earth can we do? It's just like your gang, but God hasn't spoken to us like he did to you.' I wasn't sure whether she was feeling resentful towards us or God, or was just plain upset.

Then someone came up with a plan. It was one of those special moments when a single voice seems to speak the thoughts of everybody. 'Let's go and pray under that mural, where that young man died. I think that's what God wants us to do.'

Celia, with Gaynor on her arm, led the group towards the steps under the gable end. The dominating mural got bigger and bigger, and I have rarely felt more scared, even though I would be gone in the morning – unlike my new friends from the estate.

'See that chip van?' queried Celia. 'Over there on the road?'

'Yes?'

'That's where the Loyalists watch from. All the time. It's their estate and they've got it sewn up. They'll be watching us now.'

'Now?' I answered nervously. 'At nine o'clock at night?'

'Oh yes. It's their patch, you see.'

I stood with the brave group of 20 or so Northern Ireland Christians in that dire place as together we prayed for God's presence to overcome the evil and break through. Out of the safe building they had trooped, and into the midst of the battlefield – or so it seemed. I had so much admiration for this group of ordinary Christians. They were not hiding behind a religious facade, but facing the pains and problems of this world. How much they had to teach us.

Later, a Church of Ireland minister had taken Mary to one side. 'When we heard your story about angels protecting your church building, we knew it was for us as well. We had been experiencing so much mindless vandalism, so the whole church council got together and we placed angels around our church.'

Mary looked vaguely wary. 'It was just what God told us to do. It's not magic, you know.'

'Well, whatever,' he replied, tossing off Mary's comment. 'The vandalism decreased almost straightaway. But it wasn't so much that,' he stated unequivocally. 'The amazing thing was the neighbour.'

'The neighbour?' Mary queried, feeling slightly confused.

'He saw them,' declared the minister. 'He came up to me one day and said, "Do you know you've got angels around your church?" I told him that we'd prayed for them. "Well, I saw them," he said to me. "One at each end, and taller than the church, they were. Towering right over it. Never seen anything like it. Right there through my living room window. Amazing!" That's what he said, Mary. Clear as day.' The minister looked directly at Mary and gave her a slight smile as if he were about to share a confidence. 'Asian man he was. Just been converted and he goes to the city centre church, he tells me. Now what do you think of that?'

Even more poignant was a book recently published by our local historical society.[2] The researcher had discovered that back in the early nineteenth century there was a violent, godless group called the Quinton Mob. The writer tells of 'the persecution suffered by the primitive Methodists' through 'the Quinton Mob', who were clearly a lawless, desperate group, sharing the same name as the group that persecuted our church some two centuries later. How astonishing, and spiritually significant, that such a group had held sway over an area for 200 years.

* * *

I suddenly realised the hymn was finished, and having adjusted my robes sat down with that thought of 200 years of history repeating itself. How often it seems that physical happenings in this world have some sort of spiritual root. Yet even in the midst of these poignant reflections, I was profoundly aware of being at the centre of religious 'stuff'. 'What would Gaynor have thought of all this?' I asked myself. 'And what about Zac and Dana sitting out there on the hard pews?' They were estate folk to the core and all their personal history would surely rebel against this 'middle-class' religious ritual. Was I not merely adding to the alienation of the church from ordinary life and normal people? How many people knew what 'canon' meant anyway? I'd already suffered all the lame jokes about being 'shot' and 'thick as a cannon ball'.

---

[2] Anthony N. Rosser, *The Quinton and Round About* (Quinton Historical Society, 1999).

I thought again that maybe my very involvement was merely an egocentric fop to the establishment. After all, my calling was to follow the crucified Christ and not merely to conform, and perhaps add, to a religious system that prevents people getting to the true heart of faith. Jesus said to the Pharisees, 'You shut the kingdom of heaven in men's faces.'[3] Heaven forbid that today's church might inadvertently do the same thing by making the observance of the system more important than the accessibility of the gospel.

However, I knew what Mary would say if I dared to comment. She would patiently close her eyes and explain as if I were a primary school child: 'Wallace, don't you remember the word God has given us about this? You know as well as I do that it's your calling to work from the inside. Well?'

Perhaps I could look superior and say, 'Excuse me, but I'm a canon now. You will have to make an appointment!' If only I were brave enough . . .

* * *

Mary and I snuggled up together that night (I'd decided not to ask her to call me 'Canon'!) and talked about the day. 'Mary, I still don't like all this religious establishment. You know – all that dressing up and ceremonial. What does it mean?'

'Don't give me that,' she smiled. 'I saw you in the cathedral looking as proud as a peacock.'

'But even if it does make me feel special, it's all so pompous and pretentious. Do you know what I mean?'

---

[3] Matthew 23:13.

She sighed in mock despair. 'You don't mean all the ritual. What you mean is the "stuff" that Jesus condemned.'

'Stuff? Cannabis or Ecstasy? Which do you mean?' I interjected with a smile, thinking of Zac and Dana, the ex-users who had supported me through the service.

'You know fine well what I mean,' she replied, poking me in the ribs, and then continued, 'Remember that mural in Belfast? What you hate is the "stuff" that compromises faith. Pharisaism and bigotry. Like I said, the "stuff" that Jesus condemned: the system, when it gets out of hand and becomes an end in itself.'

I gave a false snore in reply. But she was not fooled.

'Non-authentic religion is what you mean. It's the ecclesiastical power games that you can't stand.'

I gave another snore.

* * *

As the night grew silent, I reflected on what had been a good day. But I still thought of Gaynor, as well as Zac and Dana: people with messed-up lives, whom Jesus had met with in a supernatural and awesome way. I didn't want them systemised by religion. I wanted them to retain the powerful freshness of uncompromising faith. Changed lives are what ministry is all about. And even though my mind yelled at the sheer pride of ecclesiastical preferment, I believed God wanted me to be on the 'inside'. I knew that God's hand was on my being made a canon. In some small way, I believed it would give me opportunities to speak up for the Gaynors and Zacs of this world against the 'man-made' institutional systems of religion. I remembered how Jesus himself had spoken against the 'yeast of the Pharisees and Sadducees'[4] as he broke down the terrible barriers that had been erected between establishment and people.

As I stretched out in the warmth of the bed, unable to sleep because of the adrenaline of the day, I inwardly reflected, 'Wouldn't it be wonderful if all the "religion" of the church could be cleared out so that authentic faith could flourish?' In my sleepy mind I speculated, 'Surely that's the way to move mountains.'

[4] Matthew 16:6.

2

Zac's World

Without faith it is impossible to please God. (Hebrews 11:6)

The very next morning, as the new canon proudly emerged from the vicarage, Zac and Dana were waiting for me.

'That dealer came again this morning,' Zac announced without one thought of my new 'position'. Ecclesiastical preferment was a nonsense to him, even though he liked 'his vicar' to be fussed over. 'Still wants the money. Pushed me back into the door, he did. Until Dana came along and gave him a bit of mouth. As if I had any money. What a joke!'

His wife piped up, 'I don't know how much Brett owes him for the stuff, but there isn't much he can do about it from prison, is there?'

'Yeah, but it's me who's being threatened,' Zac retorted. 'And they want to let Brett out with one of those radar things round his ankle. What happens then? That's what I want to know. And he'll still be taking the stuff – you know that.'

'Tell him he can't use our address,' said Dana. She turned to me, 'If they let him out, he has to give an address, see? He wants to come to us again. But it's not right. All the old fun and games will just start up again.' Dana looked at her pained husband. 'I keep telling him that, but will he listen? Always wants it his way, he does.'

Zac's reply rose quite a few decibels: 'But he'll just go back to thieving again for the money to get it. And he is our son, after all . . .'

There on the doorstep, for all the world to see, was the new canon of the Church of England listening to an increasingly noisy 'discussion' about a young man who abused heroin, and then abused the neighbourhood through burglary to support the spiralling cost. Earlier in his emotionally traumatised life, Brett had encountered Jesus at a Christian children's camp. He'd come back to Birmingham full of it, and in a few short weeks his parents had left a life of debauchery and started to follow the Lord. God had dramatically rescued them, but their son was still caught up in all the consequences. But we believe that one day the Lord will call his name again.

In the church, I lit a candle to give a physical focus as we prayed for Brett. As so often happens when we bring these awful situations before God, the despair gradually evaporated and the argument and self-blame died down. 'What do people do without God in these situations?' asked Zac with a shake of his head. 'I'd just lose it.'

As we quietly prayed together, a gentle sense of supernatural warmth seemed to envelop us. I saw tears start to fall from Dana's eyes. God was surely there in the midst of it, carrying Zac and Dana. That is what faith is all about: God in the midst; warm, welcoming Father God, alive and vital.

Later they went out with a smile on their faces, ready to face the dealer or the prison visit or the scorn of neighbours. This was the real world of council estate culture. And this is where Jesus is.

However, the needy of this world are not only the outwardly needy with obvious problems. Many enabled Christians get caught up in the affairs of this world and entrapped in the religious system. Such people are 'inwardly needy', as they fail to develop a powerful faith dynamic, yet often they exercise church influence and even leadership.

At the same time, I despair of Christians who harp on about being fed and wallow in sitting 'under teaching' yet show little interest in *doing*. I can remember no command of our Lord to sit Sunday after Sunday being fed, but I can point to many, many places that tell us to 'give and it shall be given unto you' and to become 'doers of the word'. Recently, in Birmingham, a strong teaching church that attracted many enabled, professional Christians imploded because of internal problems. Part of the result has been enabled Christians being spread far and wide to more 'needy' fellowships, where some have become doers rather than growing obese with simply sitting and nodding assent. This is brilliant – even though God does raise up churches that teach in peer groups and they have an importance.

Some months later, I took Zac to his first meeting of Deanery Synod. He was developing in his Christian faith and wanting to get involved in the 'wider church'. The two of us sat primly in a beeswax-scented ancient pew surrounded by the religious artifacts of 'middle England' Christianity. My Christian friend looked very 'estate' against the background of 40 or so suits, dog collars and smart outfits. The Church of England, at its meeting of the twelve or so parishes and various chaplains and so forth of the 'deanery', makes a statement about itself: white, older and middle class.

I whispered smilingly to Zac, 'The vicar here gets expenses you wouldn't believe – an entertainment allowance for wine and smoked salmon.' Some time before he had told me of a

£120 dinner party he'd held for a few of his well-heeled parishioners. 'They're used to the best wine, so that's what I have to give them,' he'd falteringly explained.

Zac looked uncertain. 'So what's this all about? Why are we here?'

'They want to discuss us joining up a bit with the Methodists. What do you think of that?'

'What do I care? It's the same Lord, isn't it? What's the difference?'

He was so right.

The meeting started with a crisis. Or at least what the powers that be viewed as a crisis. Were we quorate? Were there enough people to make decisions according to the rules and regulations? After 20 minutes of comment and counter-comment, the meeting continued. Zac just sat and looked. I wondered what was going on in his mind.

A vague prayer led us to the great debate of the evening. Should we be 'organically' joined with the Methodist Church? An excellent Indian speaker told of the union back home, and Zac looked animated and pleased. He understood the stories and the point of the talk. Then the meeting went pear-shaped as dog-collar/suit/outfit brigade debated historical and legalistic points. Backwards and forwards it swayed, with able and literate speakers informing us of various points of order and 'Porvoo statements'.

It ceased, at that moment, to communicate with Zac's world. I saw his eyes glaze over; perhaps thinking of his Brett languishing in a small, clinical prison cell. Yet surely this was also Zac's church. I was glimpsing how alien the churchy system was for my friend – and for the millions of Zacs who form the great unchurched mass of our nation. He could no sooner own this meeting than fly to the moon. It was certainly not a question of intelligence, but of formal education, culture and clique. The great debates of Christianity are profoundly applicable to all Christian men and women, and, as Wesley showed with his 'classes', can be made available to all. But our synod was simply not accessible to Zac. No more, I fear, than are many church services throughout our land. No doubt, as the synod, they are worthy and thoughtful, but they are inaccessible. Religious 'stuff' thrives on inaccessibility and can bounce people away from the living God.

Zac loves Jesus and wants his church to thrive. I have no doubt that most at that synod meeting felt a similar urge. Indeed, most in our churches up and down the nation have the same inner urge from the Holy Spirit. It's a question of sorting ourselves out so the system doesn't become the barrier to people meeting with the Lord. How devastated most of that synod group would have felt to know they had alienated Zac; that their synod was a million miles away from Zac's world. Yet in truth, that is so often the consequence of our system. So let's change it! Let's make our meetings and our services and our Christianity accessible to all: Zac or royalty, black or white, professor or labourer. Each of us has a part to play in God's kingdom as we tear down barriers so that we are all one in Christ Jesus.

Zac had the last word. 'What planet are those people on?' he asked me on the way home. 'Will I become like that if I get involved? I don't fancy that very much.'

He'd hit the nail on the head. Within our British culture, there is a potential and actual enslavement of leaders and congregation members to a church philosophy that owes more to religious protocol and folk religion than to the gospel of Jesus Christ. Most religious people at the time of Jesus had buried the spirituality and faith of the Old Testament beneath layers of an institutionalised creed. 'Be on your guard against the yeast of the Pharisees and Sadducees,' said Jesus.[1] It was a terrible truth that the temple and synagogue leaders alienated people from God rather than drawing them towards him. Zac was inadvertently suggesting the same thing: 'Is it about religion or about God?'

My mind drifted to early days when I knew nothing about faith and it had been easy to scorn all institutionalised religion and superficially agree with Karl Marx. Something about the opiate of the people, wasn't it?

[1] Matthew 16:6.

3
God's Workmanship

> For we are God's workmanship, created in Christ Jesus to do good works, which God prepared in advance for us to do. (Ephesians 2:10)

In my childhood, I always saw the church as an institution – rather like the nearby Victorian 'mental' asylum building that seemed to spawn small groups of quiet and slightly strange institutionalised inmates. When I was about ten, I remember seeing an old priest standing outside his Victorian church building. Behind him, and slightly ajar, was the massive oak, iron-clad doorway. I peered round him, but all was dark and sort of spooky and chilly, like the entrance to a dungeon in my childish mind. The priest himself looked like a giant in his skirts, emphasised by a very large gut! And in his mouth, dangling from his lower lip, was a Woodbine cigarette. And just as I was looking at him, the ash fell off the fag onto his enlarged stomach. He made a sort of grunt, and rubbed it in with a careless flick of his hand. Then he turned and walked back into the darkness, and the door clanged shut. God was like that in my childish mind: elderly, cold, separate, Victorian and slightly strange.

But into that over-riding image God was planting other impressions, because God is in the life of every Christian, even before they have taken the human step of commitment. On the way to school one day, I inadvertently wandered out into the busy main road and a car missed me by a millisecond. I suppose that's a fairly normal experience in today's world, yet it has always helped me, by God's grace, to understand that God is the Master of time; and that it was no accident that there wasn't an accident.

Another time, I'd discovered my father's air pistol hidden in our attic at home in Newcastle, and for a while I became preoccupied with taking out the glass in our neighbour's greenhouse. Why? For destructive excitement mainly, but also because he was, in my imagination, a fusty old religious person because he was a Salvation Army captain (even though, to the best of my memory, I'd never met him). The day came when my father discovered what his son had been up to, and I was frog-marched to the neighbour's house. Three things stand out. First, I had to say sorry. Secondly, my father paid the price by giving my neighbour a crisp, new ten shilling note. After all, I had no money, so there was no way I could pay. Thirdly, the neighbour was brilliant – the opposite of my 'religious' perception. In a way, it was a mini-gospel – the repentance, the price being paid, and the acceptance – and it's something I've always carried with me. Of course God knew all this right from the womb and even before I was formed![1]

Yet the outward perception of a musty institution that had little to do with reality remained with me. The church establishment lived in a parallel universe. Who cared, except for some religious old folk and the vicar? And his job was simply to sort things like weddings and baptisms. Life was to be lived: the job had to be tackled and the family had to be raised.

---

[1] Psalm 119:73.

Until one evening: that evening when my mother's disembodied, subdued voice spoke quietly over the telephone: 'Wallace, there's no easy way to tell you this, but your dad has a brain tumour. He's got to go into Addenbrooks Hospital in Cambridge for an operation, but they don't hold out much hope.'

The words entered my brain, but had no effect. What was she telling me? Surely Mum wasn't saying that my dad was dying? How could that be so? He was never ill. Anyway, death had no place in my life. It was something that only happened to grandparents or other people.

'It's only the size of a pea,' her voice continued, 'but it's right behind his eyes. They'll have to remove his eyes to operate.' Was this *my* dad she was talking about? 'The doctor says it's why he's become so irritable. Had you noticed that?' Well no, I hadn't really. My dad was just my dad! 'You'll need to come over to Cambridge. See him . . . you know – before . . .' But hang on a moment. I had to go to work. I soon discovered he couldn't hang on . . .

The funeral director's parlour was filled with the dead body of my father. I touched him. The body was cold. I'd never seen a dead body before. But where was my dad? Where had he gone to? Clearly this thing in front of me was only a shell. And pretty soon it would be burned up. What happened to people when they died? I hadn't the slightest clue. I'd never thought about it before. What did the church have to say about a dead body? My past screamed at me, 'Nothing at all.' And, strangely, the funeral service built on my prejudices. It appeared to have nothing to do with God. It just happened. I was fitted into the socio-religious system for death, and that was that. At the time, the folk religion system anaesthetised me. It raised no questions and offered no answers – only the bland comfort of ritual and getting it over with.

It was months afterwards that God thoughts started to rage through my mind. If my dad was nothing but dust and ashes, what did that say about me? Was life merely a cul-de-sac leading to death and oblivion? And if so, what was the point? Better to get it all over with. But if God were really God, where could I find him? My mind struggled with the ever enlarging question for about two years, through escalating ambition and new job and better job, together with house moves. But nothing really satisfied.

Mary, as always, provided the way forward. 'Seen this leaflet, Wallace? There's a new church being set up. Why don't we . . . ?'

'Yeah, I don't mind, if you want to.' I wanted to really. But it was good to make it seem that Mary was the reason. Wasn't church a woman thing anyway?

'And we might meet some of the folk from round here. It's all right for you, off to your new job every morning, but what about me? School journeys then sitting around the house.'

'You? Sitting around? Don't make me laugh. But you're right, we need to get out more. This Sunday then?'

Mary looked thoughtful. 'The children will be surprised. Wonder what they will think?'

We met Shona there. There was nothing special about her, except that she wasn't the least bit religious and she loved Jesus. Vibrantly and joyfully. She reminded me somehow of the Salvation Army man in Newcastle.

'God sorted me out a parking space again this morning,' she smiled at the little group that was meeting to talk about life, the universe and all that. Perhaps a forerunner of Alpha.

'Excuse me? A parking space? Surely Shona didn't think that God was going to change the whole direction of the universe and the whole understanding of human free will simply for the momentary convenience of her parking space? I looked at her with cynical and humorous indignation. Surely she wasn't asking me to believe that – even if there was a God? Anyway, wouldn't he have enough to do? Why couldn't he heal a few people with cancer or stop drought in Ethiopia if he was that interested?

However, one day I put it to the test and went with her into Sheffield. She prayed in the car, but what a different sort of prayer! No head bowed or hands together. She simply chatted with God! Unbelievable! And it worked. That was the sort of religion I wanted!

Shona's faith helped so much to bring my two long years of searching to an end. It facilitated my step in faith, so that one Tuesday evening in my Sheffield home, I could and did ask Jesus into my heart.[2] And he came! He proved himself to be a person, not merely an institution or a system. A divine person who was delighted to call me his child. A person who is, paradoxically, big enough to be outside the universe, yet spiritual enough to reign within my soul. I became a born-again Christian, experiencing the presence of the Almighty. Why, even church took on a different feel. I actually *needed* to go to the 7 am service in the cold, permanently wintery church!

A few months later, I even found myself at a Pentecostal healing meeting. 'In the name of Jesus, be made whole!' shouted the anointed minister as he thumped his hand down on one woman's head. The wheelchair seemed to shudder as the woman lifted her arthritically twisted limbs to a sort of standing position. And then, as I stood just two feet away viewing the whole situation with sceptical eyes, her limbs straightened, her body rose in height and her face was transformed from pain to joy. God had healed her,

[2] See *Angels on the Walls.*

dramatically and fully, before my very eyes. And it happened in a church.

'I want to be a minister of the gospel, just like him,' I thought.

Yet God, I knew, was calling me not just to be part of that living church of all Christians of all times. That would have been easy and allowed me to nurture my prejudices. He was calling me to the Anglican ministry. He was calling me to travel deeply into the ecclesiastical system . . .

4

The Prison Bars

> They read from the Book of the Law of God, making it clear and giving the meaning so that the people could understand what was being read. (Nehemiah 8:8)

I felt full. I was going out to proclaim Jesus. My college training church awaited me, my sermon was tucked carefully in my inside pocket and I was ready.

Of course, I also felt vaguely stupid. I had to wear robes for the first time in public. In the naivety of the working out of my call to be a vicar, it had never occurred to me that I would be expected to dress up and preach from a pulpit, and, more to the point, perform like a vicar to some unknown congregation before and after the service.

The night before, I'd stood in full robes in front of a mirror and practised. First I tried looking sombre and then speaking out with flowing gestures. That was easy because the gear itself made a statement. Then I tried looking holy. Someone had told me that if you focus your eyes at an indeterminate distance from the person you are speaking to, and at the same time soften the look to make your eyes serene, it gives you that holy look. Was that the look needed when offering a limp handshake at the church door tomorrow? I felt that would surely impress my new friends!

Then a sense of the ridiculousness of it all took hold of me. So I picked up my skirts and did a quick flamboyant dance round the bedroom. The crashing noise diverted the family's attention from the TV. Mary peered questioningly round the door, so I tried my holy look on her. She merely fell about laughing! Thanks a bunch! Elizabeth, then a mere six-year-old, and now married and the mother of our grandchildren, Tabitha and Nathaniel, followed her mother into the room. She looked sort of puzzled, then asked solemnly, 'Why is my daddy dressed up like an angel?'

Still, robes were part of the package, and even a little exciting in a sort of 'lifting you out of the norm' way. And, after all, it was expected of me by church, congregation and community, or so I thought at that point. I was learning to fit into the groove of becoming an Anglican vicar.

'O Lord, open thou our lips,' chanted my training vicar in a slightly off-key tone. The elderly congregation, led by a ragtag choir of older ladies, responded in like voice, 'And our mouths shall show forth thy praise.'

Mary raised her eyes at me and then nodded an unspoken comment towards our children. She said afterwards, 'At least they could go out to Sunday school to get away from it all. They were quite pleased really, because as far as I can see, they were drip fed with chocolate to keep them sweet!'

'And what did you think of my sermon?' I asked her nervously. I was aware that even I had felt bored halfway through it. 'I'm only on page two of my four pages,' I'd thought in panic. The words seemed timid and cold, the content totally dry. The one story I used just didn't work. Redness crept round from the back of my neck, my whole body temperature went up several degrees and profound embarrassment swept through me. The pulpit became my prison, the robes my shackles and the notes blurred.

'Do you want truth or fiction?' questioned my thoughtful wife.

'Well, everybody at the church door seemed happy about it,' I said defensively.

'Maybe they'd fallen asleep then,' she commented sagely.

I was being introduced to the system. To be a Church of England minister necessitates certain methods of being, fulfilling historic expectations of various groups of people. Now I was fairly well used to sharing about Jesus to a normal group of people, wearing normal clothes and communicating in a normal friendship way with talk and response. But this was the churchy method, which lifted everything out of the normal. For me, this would become the normal.

Later, our whole family went to have lunch with the vicar and his wife. As we sat down in the untidy dining room, the children were showing their frustration at being 'seen and not heard' in Sunday school. Jeremy was muttering, 'Mum, I don't want to go to that church again,' and Elizabeth was screaming wildly while being 'innocently' chased by an imagined crab claw in her other brother's hand. 'Nip, nip!' I heard clearly from the hallway. Nor were our young chocaholics hungry. In fact they were soon hissing at Mary about the liver, 'I don't like that!' and making castles with the cabbage.

As Mary sought to maintain the veneer of a loving Christian family, I noticed something was very wrong, and even I could almost feel the resentment seething between the couple. It suddenly struck me that the house wasn't just untidy but dirty. Albert leaned over to me as Dinah went to fetch the tapioca and said, 'She's not so well, you know. Depression.' He looked at me knowingly, as the children learned the dreadful truth about the pudding.

'You see, it hasn't worked out,' he told me flatly some months later. 'It was all right when I was in the London City Mission. We had this flat two floors up, and many's the time Dinah had to step over drunks in the doorway.' He blinked his eyes in tragic and nostalgic weariness. 'And we never had enough food. But you know, we never went without.' A slight smile formed in the edges of his eyes, momentarily transforming him into a much younger man. 'You see, we used to pray, Dinah and I. We used to pray for our food. And I remember one night, just as we thought we had no dinner, the local butcher rang the bell and left us a load of lamb chops. What a blessing! Right out of the blue.' The smile was full now. Those were the days.

Ministry had not worked out well for Albert and Dinah. It had become a sort of prison; just as much as the pulpit had for me during my first sermon. Here they were, grossly disappointed, hope nearly all gone. They were disappointed with God, yet unable to express such a heretical thought. Their church was merely rambling on, with people getting older and financial problems becoming overwhelming.

'When I came into the ministry, I said I would never do a lot of things,' said Albert sadly. 'I said I would never baptise a baby of unbelievers, but I've done literally thousands. What can I do? It's what everybody expects. I said I would never hold jumble sales to pay the church bills, but what can I do? The first thing that happened when I arrived was a bill for £5,000 to repair the church pinnacles. I didn't even know what pinnacles were, but I soon learned. I said I wouldn't let any church of mine be stuck in the 1950s so that young people were alienated. But Clara won't have any truck with what she calls 'choruses', and all the folk seem to agree with her. What can I do? She's been the organist here for quarter of a century.'

Albert leaned over and touched my arm with disarming frankness. The pain was so visible it almost shouted at me. 'I said I would never become the stereotypical vicar, but here's Dinah all over the place and all I do is work harder and harder, and I'm just irritable all the time with her.'

Yet in many ways Albert was such a wonderful man. He had so much love to give and still yearned to speak of Jesus. He was a tragically glorious minister of the gospel. It was my first taste of an able Christian minister imprisoned by the ecclesiastical system. He was also the man who was training me.

At the time Albert and Dinah seemed merely to be people with problems and in no way suggestive of wider issues within God's church. But since those early days I've met far too many broken and burned-out leaders of God's church – not just Anglicans, but right across all strata. Like a little Pentecostal church I came across recently, which meets in a Welsh town amid a large council estate, founded about 30 years ago by a small but dedicated group . . .

* * *

'How does it feel to you?' queried the minister's wife, Lily. Her husband, Leslie, nodded at the question as Mary and I prodded and poked our way around the empty building. This was the sort of time when I wish I had immediate insight, enabling me to give a profound answer to which they would nod, amazed at my perception. Actually, I was feeling cold and in dire need of a cup of tea.

Mary replied, with awareness I longed for, 'I'd love to know the history of this church. Especially how it all got started.'

'Funny you should say that,' spoke out Lily. She had a soft-spoken manner that fitted perfectly with her bright eyes. Here was a person I could trust and enjoy working alongside. Surely she would be loved by her husband's congregation. 'This church was funded and organised by a man called Randle. He put everything into it.'

Leslie then echoed his wife's words, 'Put the lot into it, he did. And I don't mean just money.'

Lily continued as if her husband had never said a word. 'He financed and sorted out most everything like the furnishings, chairs, organ and so on. He was treasurer, leader of the social group and taught Sunday school.'

'He was the treasurer, see?' repeated Leslie. 'And elder as well, unfortunately – for years and years until he died, then his son became an elder himself. Like a family affair, see?'

Lily continued the double conversation: 'Randle was our founder really. When he was dying, he directed the whole system from his hospital bed. His family were the core. Still are, for that matter.' Lily's expression changed to one of struggle.

'Everything revolved round him for years and years,' Leslie took up the story. I ungraciously wondered whether his wife would echo his words. 'Even on his deathbed, he made his son promise to continue his work, see? He teaches the Sunday school now. That was Randle's system.'

I waited for the 'see?' at the end of his sentence, but he merely paused for a moment and then continued, 'Mind you, Lily and I, well, we really doubt if his heart is in it. Or even if he's a proper Christian. Church has become like a shrine to Randle's way of doing things. The church is like a memorial to him, see?'

Lily smiled bleakly. 'Tried to move the chairs around the other week and somebody came up to me and said, "You mustn't do that. It's not how Randle had it." You see how it is?'

Of course I saw. Plain as a pikestaff. Randle had set up a system of being church relevant to his heyday, and here was this small Pentecostal church, built to focus on God's Holy Spirit and his gifts of today, staggering into the twenty-first century! No doubt there had been light emanating from the set-up in the past, but . . .

It is a deep frustration. The church has such a wonderful, life-changing message, yet in many places people are confined by systems rather than released by the Spirit to be full of Jesus. Power groups, which certainly don't mean to be power groups, often dominate. And whereas the church can offer a fine, organised, superficial welcome on a Sunday morning, it is a very different matter from being authentically welcomed into the innards. For many people, 'church' is a disempowering rather than releasing word. Simply mention the word 'church' and see eye contact broken and the immediate creation of an atmosphere. Or worse still, the speaker is mentally categorised as being slightly odd, naive and unworldly.

People talk glibly about renewal and even revival. I want to talk about a church that is fractured and hurting. Of course, for some, their local church is dynamic and thriving. Indeed some churches are authentically mission minded with a real heart for the gospel. However, in my experience, many churches are simply a clique of elderly people conspiring, often non-comprehendingly, against the twenty-first century.

How can we stand up and bellow to a broken world that they need the Lord and they need to come along to church when they perceive with the eyes of truth the culturally off-putting religious rite that many churches truly offer, with hardly a hint of vibrant spirituality and little authentic human friendliness. 'I don't want any of that emotional stuff or those dreadful choruses in "my" church,' mutters the founding elder.

How is it that we have often allowed the ecclesiastical system, of whatever churchmanship or hue, to become king of the church, and the true King to be pushed to the margins? More than that, society in our country has an underlying image of the church. Its corporate mind sees a hidebound, narrow-minded and even – in certain places – dangerous and bigoted group of people meeting in an archaic building.

The church has to face further problems in that postmodern people have few absolutes, so that what is right for you is right. The pick 'n' mix spirituality and therefore morality, especially of the rising generation, abhors the concepts of obedience and servanthood that are the keynotes of Christian discipleship. Add to that the folksy expectations of baptisms, weddings and funerals, where words have lost their meaning and truth becomes victim, and society ends up seeing the church as history.

I was soon to discover for myself that building up a local church to break the bounds of systemised religion is a truly backbreaking task. Jesus appeared to make it all so simple. He simply preached the gospel. But then it wasn't quite so simple, was it? It ended up in Gethsemane and Calvary as he spoke totally of God, following in the tradition of the great prophets as they spoke of a people and a nation turning their backs on God[1] to such an extent that systemised religion could prosper. Think for a moment of Moses: how, the moment he went back up the mountain of God, the people

[1] 2 Chronicles 29:6.

ran amok and started to worship the golden calf, which did not demand repentance, commitment and faith, but rather offered debauchery and revelry. The golden idol still thrives, if in a different form, calling people away from authentic faith to systemised religion. And the devil stands and laughs, as well he might.

Returning to those early days at Oak Hill Theological College, I have a good and grateful memory of Albert and Dinah. Despite their personal needs they welcomed and helped this arrogant young trainee vicar and his family. In the midst of their troubles they were still lovely people of God. The system may have messed up their ministry, but I can, even looking back some 30 years later, still perceive Jesus in them. I have a lot to thank them for.

Over the following years, as I was ordained deacon and then priest at Leicester Cathedral, I kept my head down as I sought to work out my calling of being a vicar. After my time as curate and priest-in-charge at Oadby, I was called to head up a little council estate church in Birmingham, where I was to meet with those 'angels on the walls'.

It was to be quite a few years before God took my early experiences of people like Albert and Dinah and moulded them together with Lily and Leslie and many others, so setting me on the pathway towards understanding the 'mountain' of slavery to the system that has to be overcome by the dynamic of the mustard seeds of faith.

In the meantime, God had charged me with the business of building up our little congregation on our three difficult council estates. That was the job of the moment . . .

[illegible]

[illegible] God. The person may have [illegible]

Then the following morning [illegible]

[illegible]

5

Seeds of Positiveness

'Do whatever he tells you.' (John 2:5)

We were finishing our first years at Quinton. The work was going reasonably well: people were being saved and baptised with the Holy Spirit, and the church was growing in stature. The faith days of placing 'angels on the walls' were now a memory rather than a present reality, but all in all it was going well.

Mary and I were at a conference – something to do with fire for revival. Now I am not very good at conferences, especially at the meal table. I have to either put on a total extrovert face and be the life and soul of the group, or else retreat into oblivion. Whichever way, I rarely have the confidence just to be myself. And why is that everybody except me seems so successful? They come up with stories of great happenings with thousands (or so it seems) saved, as well as dynamic forward-thrusting, proactive churches. I was feeling weaker and weaker and trying to justify my little council estate church. I sensed mine was not the place where the called-for 'fire of revival' would break out, nor could anyone afford the 'required' trip to Toronto or Pensacola.

But there was one exciting thought that rose to the surface. The speaker asked, 'What is your dream?' Now he didn't mean 'What weird story did you find yourself in when you woke up sweating in the middle of last night?' or 'Who's heard from God in a spiritual dream?' – at least I don't think he did. What he asked for was a purpose statement; a *raison d'être*. Rene Descartes said, 'I think, therefore I am.' The speaker wanted to know 'You are a church leader therefore . . .'

Mary nudged me gently as the talk progressed. 'Are you OK?' she hissed, thinking she was waking me up.

I drew a little picture of a man with a speech bubble emerging from his head. 'My Dream' it said inside.

'Go back to sleep,' she whispered with a slight smile.

Afterwards I explained the bubble. 'I know what my dream is. St B's has to be an authentic church. It's not about excellent religious practice or bums on seats or a name or even 'fire of revival'. It's simply being a church that is in tune with God and doing God-things.'

'I know what you mean,' added Mary, starting to feel the challenge. 'A church where faith is understood and practised. Is that what you mean?'

'Yes,' I answered. 'Small[1] or big, it doesn't matter. What matters is that we are full of faith and full of the Lord.'

'That's good,' she answered and nodded her head. 'I agree. So why don't you stop getting so het up about being a success and let's just get on with it? After all, God's called us here, and it's his church, and our job is to find out what he wants us to do here.'

'But not just looking backwards at our faith stories of old, Mary, so we will still be telling the "angels" story from our rocking chairs. But faith for today. What is God going to tell us to do *today*?'

---

[1] Zechariah 4:10.

'I agree,' she nodded again.

'What? Right twice in a row? This must be a record,' I thought, but didn't say so!

When God brings something to the surface, he always has a reason. And, sure enough, a short time afterwards Mary and Richard Chamberlain[2] came back to St B's for a flying visit. We had hardly sat down for coffee when Mary C, eyes shining brightly, burst out, 'The Lord is calling us to go to Denmark.'

She looked at her husband who nodded agreement. 'Copenhagen. The Lord has told us to go to Copenhagen and tell the Danes about Jesus. And we've been asked to build up a Bible college there.'

Now Mary and Richard are two dynamic people of faith, and their straightforward, no-nonsense faith always fires my faith after I have overcome my cynical response pattern. 'The Lord has *told* you? Don't you mean you *think* God has told you?'

Richard merely looked bemused. 'Wallace, it's what he wants us to do. That's it. And that's what we are going to do.'

I pressed the point. 'And how much Danish can you speak?' And then added with unforgivable sarcasm, 'Or maybe you think he will give you the gift of tongues in Danish.' Richard continued to smile his 'faith smile'. 'And what about money? What about your children? What about . . .?' My voice tailed off because I was the one in the wrong, and Mary was looking at me in that sort of pitying, eyes half-closed way. The fact is God had spoken, and it was wonderful that here were two people who would go to the ends of the earth at the slightest beckoning of the hand of God.

'Why Denmark then, Mary?' I asked in a quieter voice.

---

[2] See *Angels on the Walls.*

'Well, we believe the Lord has called us to get a coach rigged out for evangelism and then take it to Copenhagen to share the gospel.' The light of faith touched her whole being as she said passionately, 'It'll be called "the King's Coach", and we'll train up the Danes in the Bible college to share the gospel alongside us.'

'Well, sounds like a good idea,' I cautiously answered in an unconvincing tone. And then, mostly to change the subject: 'How are your children getting on, anyway?'

I thought that the faith drama of the Chamberlains would leave me as they left for Norwich en route to Denmark. But God had other plans. A few nights later I had the other sort of dream: a powerful dream I knew instantly was from God. I was handing over a sizeable cheque to Mary and Richard for the purchase of their 'King's Coach'. I clearly remember asking God in my dream, 'How am I to raise the thousands of pounds? The church is on the edge of insolvency at the moment.'

He answered, 'Wallace, I want you to ask the church to do it – to buy it.'

'Excuse me?' I dreamily replied. 'But we have no money and the people are too poor to think of the evangelisation of Copenhagen. Anyway, we have enough problems round here!'

'Tell your people to stop buying food for a week; to live on what they have in their cupboards. And don't worry. It will all work out to my glory.'

Tell people to stop buying food for a week! Tell them to live on what they have in their cupboards!

'Honestly, that's what I think God said to me,' I told Mary as we sat drinking our breakfast coffee and discussing Copenhagen. 'I can understand calling us to a night of prayer or even to a gift day. But I've never heard the like of this before. What do I say, for goodness' sake? "God wants you to stop eating!"'

'Now don't exaggerate,' replied Mary. 'We could do that – live on what we have in the cupboard for a week. And, I dare say, so could most other people in the church. It would be a boring week – dried pasta shells and those old rice grains from that tin up there – but we could do it.'

* * *

The Clent Hills, just to the west of Birmingham, looked so beautiful in the watery sun the following Saturday morning. However, the pre-Christmas winter wind was starting to bite; even the puddles protected themselves with thin layers of ice. My favourite 'prayer path' was beckoning, and I felt pleased, as usual, that so few people knew about it. This was my personal space, and I had thoughts to be thought and a talk to prepare for the morning.

As I forged my way through the icy ruts, my mind could not leave the Copenhagen situation alone. How amazing, I considered, for a 'poor and needy' church on a council estate in Birmingham to finance evangelistic outreach to such a place – and beyond, into places like Poland and the old Eastern European bloc. This was surely the kernel of a faith adventure from the Lord. Yes, it was right, I determined in my mind and soul. With a new determination I brushed aside the soaking branches overhanging my path. Faith meant breaking free of normal, systemised ways and exploring God things. Yes, it was right; proactive, as they would say today. And that's what we needed to be: proactive in faith things.

I went on further as the sun started to abandon the day – and further into my mind as well. I reflected that religion is often so amazingly reactionary. It's as if we are happy just to maintain; to keep things going. We Western Christians have become indolent fat cats of spiritual indifference.

I took a smuggled Mars Bar out of my pocket. The dance club that uses our church hall came to my mind. You could guarantee, come rain or shine, that the members would appear week by week. They would carefully bring their prepared gear and always turn up for special events. Why was it that Christians so often have a propensity to sink into 'doing Sunday' and that's it? No wonder society in the UK takes so little notice of us. As my car came into view, I mischievously considered that perhaps we ought to call on the dance club for help. They certainly knew how to be proactive.

* * *

I issued my challenge from the front: 'I believe the Lord wants us to finance a King's Coach for evangelism in Copenhagen.' As the words left my mouth, it became apparent that it was an anointed concept. I could almost feel the crackle of spiritual excitement. 'And look,' I continued, 'this is how much we need to give. Here's the target. Not only that, we need to buy the plane tickets in advance for Mary and Richard to come over and receive the cheque in February.'

Somebody pointed out to me after the service, 'Do you realise that's only eight weeks away, and we have Christmas to get over?' But the amazing, and spiritual, feeling of dynamic 'rightness' put everything into perspective.

The cupboard concept went down a treat. The first week

in February was to be the 'coping with what's in the larder' week. A local man who had rarely been to church before that challenging Sunday gave a week's wages. Some of the children did sponsored events at their own volition. And it was such a poignant moment when some children came forward with much of their Christmas money. One of them said, 'It's a good job that Grandad gave us money this year so we can help Richard and Mary.' How hard it must have been for them to lose their Christmas treat, yet it put all us adults to shame. A group of people who had no money except benefits decided to bring 'treasures', including some family heirlooms. Brian later went to Birmingham's Jewellery Quarter and sold them on for a good price.

As somebody commented to me on that memorable February morning when we handed the full cheque to an overwhelmed Mary and Richard: 'Wallace, it didn't fit in with common sense or anything. It was just mad. But it was brilliant. I'm so pleased to be part of a church that gets on with things like this. Thank you so much.'

I enjoyed that. I like good comments. And I like being proactive for God and faithfully 'unreasonable'. As another person commented, 'Faith is extreme and extravagant. Just like God, when he sent his Son.'

* * *

People wonder why the church is failing in our generation. It doesn't take a professor to work out the reasons. As in the times of Malachi the prophet, we live in a complacent, comfortable era. Mary and I drove past Sheffield on the M1 the other Sunday. As we looked across and down on the massive new shopping mall to the north of the city, the Sunday shoppers swarmed like ants and the vast car park was absolutely full and overflowing. People have the time, money and leisure. But church car parks are empty and uninviting. Buildings are often cold, forbidding, religious places where everything is run on a shoe-string, and even creaking, badly lined-up overhead projectors are thought to be modern technology.

More to the point, churches are not seen as 'spiritual' – the happenings mere ancient rites rather than contact with the living God. Who wants to sit on a hard, cold pew fighting with one's rebellious children when the warm, comfortable, state of the art shopping malls beckon, and the children can run relatively free, eating ice cream?

What I want is churches full of adventure and faith, where people are awake to the thrill of true spirituality; where Jesus is so evident that the very walls reverberate with his amazing and holy presence. That is what will attract our rising generation to God, not our disapproval for not keeping up the religious practices of yesterday.

As a church, we often seem to be advocating a return to how things used to be; to an unknown golden age. But surely it is we who should repent. It is we who have allowed God's wonderful church to become slothful, irrelevant and unspiritual. Full of words without power.

God's 'idea' of us purchasing a coach for evangelism in Denmark, and afterwards in Eastern Europe, had a huge effect on the people in those countries who found Christ. It also had an immense effect on our church. For that short time we became doers of the word and the vast majority of the congregation put Christ first in their home life for that 'shopless' week. And the Spirit of Jesus smiled down on us. Many people still tell that story.

But there is also a warning here. Heroic stories are good, and many churches have them, but it is the Spirit-led present that matters now. Jesus himself loved to tell the stories of the past, but he did not live in them. He proactively worked in the present and shaped the future. The amazing truth is that God has adventures in faith for every church. He has a call on every fellowship to reach out proactively in partnership with the Holy Spirit.

The system of religion, however, which the devil revels in, would rather keep everything tight and controlled and exhausting . . .

6

A Bit of a Breakdown

Restore to me the joy of your salvation and grant me a willing spirit, to sustain me. (Psalm 51:12)

On the surface all was well. So why did I feel so unsettled? Mary came towards my study and I hastily and guiltily switched off the computer game I had been playing for the last hour.

'You still in there? Do you know what the time is?' she stated rather than asked.

'What does it look like to you?' I replied stiffly. 'Work to be done, you know. A church doesn't run itself.'

'Well, what about your dinner? And you're going out again tonight, aren't you? When are we going to see each other?' Again the laconic statement rather than loving question. Or so I thought.

'In a few minutes,' I tersely replied. After another game, I inwardly decided.

All of us get caught up with things so that we lose our first love and tend towards being mechanical Christians. How many folk do you know who've become a shadow of the former live wire person of God? People who have drifted into stoic perseverance, thereby allowing the wondrous call to become a blunted memory.

That's how I was: on one side sensing good things afoot, and full of it all, yet in myself becoming short tempered for no apparent reason, and tending to brood silently over minor issues. I started to use computer games as an escape from reality. Yet to all appearances I continued as a successful minister of the gospel, and that's the impression I was quite determined should come across. I knew I needed a break away to recharge, but I felt strangely compelled to just keep on working. Mary, however, I considered, did need a holiday. She had been getting quite up tight lately. So off we went on our off-season break to Norfolk . . .

* * *

The clergy cottage smelled of damp dereliction. It was cold and stuffed full of other people's cast-off furniture. The old settee with the missing castor had to be lifted over the rutted carpet to catch the warmth of a smoky, 1950s tiled fireplace. In the bedroom the wartime utility wardrobe swayed forward on the uneven floorboards and groaned at being opened. It emitted an odour of ancient lavender – or was it mothballs?

Yet it had a sort of ethereal sense. It was an interesting place for a holiday by the sea away from our council estate vicarage; an easy place to think in – if only I had the energy to think. And I wanted desperately to think, although didn't want to admit any needs. Yet I had a sense that a lot of my inner issues emanated from an unspoken exasperation with God. All this talk about renewal and revival, but where was it? Churches of all denominations were struggling to keep going. I'd just helped close down a brilliant spiritual initiative called 'Together for Birmingham' because of lack of interest. My own church was healthy, but far from taking off. My diocese was desperately short of money, even at the present 'maintenance' level. Many of the new churches had failed to keep up with the wonderful promise of a former generation. I couldn't help wondering what was going on in the church in our country. And, more important, what the Holy Spirit was saying through it all.

On top of all these questions pounding round in my head, I felt mentally and spiritually exhausted by endless issues within my own parish. Behind us, in Birmingham, we'd left many pastoral situations still unresolved, which is how it is for a church going on with the Lord. The list seemed endless: the church member with the suicidal daughter; an arson-suspected house fire started by petrol rags through the letterbox; the church member who hit me; the chasing up of an education grant that had failed to materialise; a police station visit with an emotionally abused, disempowered church member; a deliverance session involving a free-flying sharp kitchen knife.

After a few days, Mary and I walked out along the Coastal Strand, just letting the dog run free. 'The trouble is,' she commented, 'you really are shattered. I mean, look how irritated you got last night, just over a simple game of Scrabble.'

Which I didn't want to play anyway, I thought inwardly.

The mud-flats and waterways looked beautiful as we walked into the seaside town.

'Your trouble is that you never stop. Even when you rest, you don't stop. Do you see what I mean?'

'Suppose so,' I replied. 'But it's my job! Anyway, I feel so guilty if I'm not there and available and doing things.'

We walked quietly but fairly companionably into the narrow streets, until we saw a delightful little Dickensian bookshop huddled away up an alley. Inside, time had stopped, with wonderfully awful 'sale of work' sea paintings scattered round any free space. But mostly it was books. Paradise for me.

I picked up a dusty, dog-eared old spiritual classic, George Muller's *Delighted with God.* But the title only built on my irritation. I turned aside to express my exasperation to my patient wife, but just at that very moment, a handwritten note came fluttering from the pages. As I picked it up, I saw it was addressed to an archdeacon from a friend. Interesting! So nosily I read it: 'Remember the sort of faith we used to have? We believed God could do almost anything. Literally move mountains. But sadly, like you, I've discovered you can't do that sort of faith thing nowadays. It just doesn't work and leaves everybody disappointed. I just wish it weren't so!'[1] As I read on, my interest sharpened. The letter seemed to cry out of past possibilities sullied by the deadening realities of modern life. And then I came to the last few lines: 'so sorry to hear about your troubles; that all your years of service to the church should end with a bit of a breakdown . . .' What sadness. There in that bookshop I felt like shouting out, 'It's just not fair!' All that faith reduced to 'a bit of a breakdown'. Was that what was going to happen to me? Just as it was with so many around me?

As usual Mary came to my rescue as we walked the next day along the windswept beach.

'Mary, that's just it, isn't it?' I commented into the wind.

'Excuse me?'

'That letter. That archdeacon. It sums up what's happening in the church, don't you think?'

My wife waited patiently for the holiday pontification.

'Look. There were two young men full of faith. I can

---

[1] These words depict the spirit of the note, to the best of my memory, and not the actual content.

imagine them reading those faith books and talking nineteen to the dozen about how great God is, getting really excited about things. Perhaps sitting in a pub in Cambridge or somewhere like that talking enthusiastically about the Lord, and then one of them going to the bishop and explaining how he felt a call to the ministry. But look what's happened to him. Somewhere along the line he's lost it. Perhaps even now he's sitting around wondering about faith and life . . .' Charm, our guide dog 'brood bitch' rubbed her majestic golden neck into a long-dead fish as our attention wandered. 'It's like the church today. It's just lost it. All the structure is there: buildings and synods and social awareness and liturgical correctness to preserve doctrine – even worship bands and all that stuff. But where's the dynamic faith?

'Do you remember our holiday in Tunisia? That amazing Roman amphitheatre and how we walked in the very dungeons where the Christians waited with their families to face the lions? Can you imagine the vibrant power if the church had a tenth of that kind of faith today?'

In answer to my own questions I continued, 'It's as if the church has had "a bit of a breakdown" – just like that archdeacon.' I hesitated for a moment before saying, 'Mary, I'm so sorry that I've separated myself off from you. And from God as well.' And then as an afterthought I added, 'You know, I'm beginning to think I'm part of the problem rather than part of the answer.'

* * *

On the way home, we stopped off at my sister's house. And so it was that I shared my concerns with Eileen.

'Do you see my problem, Eileen?' I asked her as we sat in her kitchen that evening. Eileen is my older sister and therefore a fount of all knowledge – plus she runs a Christian bookshop.

'Funny you should ask that. I was reading an amazing book by Peter Brierley the other day. What was it called again?'

'If you don't know, then don't look at me,' I smiled with brotherly affection.

'Anyway, he was saying that over the last decade, more than a million people in England have simply stopped attending church.' She looked at me for a reaction. 'And if you take the last two decades, Sunday attendance has dropped by well over forty per cent in the Anglican church alone. He said – and I remember this quote because it struck me at the time – that the church is "bleeding to death".'[2] She continued, 'And I remember him quoting, "Something is seriously wrong with the church. People are leaving it in droves."'[3] She looked at me with a sly smile. 'It must be you lot. You leaders,' she said and then irritatingly ruffled my hair in the manner of big sisters.

'What about the new churches then?' I asked. 'Maybe they are the answer and I just have to change sides. Maybe it's just the stodgy old establishment.'

'Hang on a second,' she replied. 'You may have a point, but I remember the book also said that growth in the new churches has slowed down dramatically.'[4]

---

[2] Dr Peter Brierley, *The Tide is Running Out* (Christian Research, 2000).

[3] Derek Tidball, a principal of London Bible College in the same book.

[4] 'The new churches, which started in the early 1970s, saw a huge growth in those first two decades . . . but only 67,000 [new people joined] in the 1990s, and this from a larger base.'

'Not only that,' I added, attempting to rumple her hair in response. 'All of us on the inside know that much of this is transfer growth anyway from the established churches of each and every denomination.'

'You lot always find an excuse, don't you?'

'Yes, dear sister,' I dutifully replied.

However, and despite sisterly love, the fate of the anonymous archdeacon impacted me mightily. Was I becoming like him? Had institutionalised religion somehow got its claws into me, dragging me away from what God wanted me to do into merely responding to the ecclesiastical system of which I had now become part?

I thought of Martin Knox. He would know what I should do. Years ago, Martin and his wife Janet had been called from Sheffield to work alongside us in St B's. He is the only senior partner of a law firm that I know of who lives on a council estate because he believes in incarnational Christian ministry.

I rang Martin from my mobile. 'Martin, I need your help. Keep Monday night free, will you?'

7
The Cobweb Trap

Where the Spirit of the Lord is there is freedom. (2 Corinthians 3:17)

'The trouble with you is that you take yourself too seriously. As if God wants you to do everything, all the time.' Martin Knox was in full flow. 'You think that because you are the vicar we "laity" are second class. You just tie yourself up in knots, always doing everything. But what do you achieve, except to wear yourself out?' He looked at me. 'Don't you know that what we want is spiritual leadership – not minister domination?' He smiled knowingly. 'Come on. We're trying to build a church that listens to God here, not just extend the ecclesiastical set-up. Look, I've made a little list of eight things that you need to sort . . .'

'Oh no. Not another "little list,"' I smilingly groaned. Then I started to quietly sing 'I've got a little list' from Gilbert and Sullivan's *Mikado*. I thought it was very fitting – until Mary looked at me.

'As I was saying,' continued Martin, 'eight things to look at if we . . .'

'We? You mean it's not just Wallace who needs to sort things?' Janet interjected to prove a point.

'That's right *we* – all of us. Eight things the "keenies"

[another Martin word] of our church need to continue to get to grips with if we are to persist in the Lord's work here – and save Wallace from a nervous breakdown,' he added with a twinkle in his eye.

Later, I went home with my mind whirling. Had I become simply a vicar, holding on to things in the false 'clerical' style Martin suggested? A diocesan meeting the following week proved the point.

I tried to stifle another yawn and looked round furtively to see who had noticed that I had nearly drifted off. However, the yawn could not be stopped, so I sort of coughed and spluttered and gave the bishop a strangled smile.

Suddenly a lay member of the diocesan committee spoke over the drone of clergy voices. Underneath his black skin, I noticed an abashed red flush, but he was determined. 'I cannot believe this meeting!' said Josiah with annoyed frustration. 'We've been here for two hours now, and you clergy have gone on and on and on, but *nobody* has even mentioned the name of Jesus! Sorting out this and that, putting the world to rights. But not one of you speaks about the Lord!'

The bishop grimaced sweetly; the rest of us shuffled slightly.

'My brothers, you're in clergy-cuckoo land!' His voice increased in pitch. 'You're nothing more than a bunch of professional religious people sorting out God. Why don't you talk about real things?'

* * *

When God proves a point, he rarely stops at one small example. I was looking forward to seeing 'Donald' again.

We'd been great friends at our theological college, often doing stupid, schoolboy things and having a good laugh in that very serious environment. Mary and I found his vicarage easily enough. Quite smart, really, with a gravelled drive and handsome front door.

Donald answered our knock.

'Brilliant to see you again,' I enthused and went forward to give him a hug.

He backed vaguely away, then changed his mind and returned my greeting, 'Very nice to see you as well, Wallace. And you, Mary, of course. Thanks for coming all this way.'

'Like your dog collar and black suit,' I remarked on the doorstep. I don't know quite why I made such an inane comment. I think I was rather shocked that Donald looked so 'vicarish', and I hadn't expected it.

'Yesss,' he replied looking equally surprised at my remark. 'Come on in, won't you? I've got the tea ready.'

Donald's living room was tasteful with Parker Knoll chairs and Sanderson furnishings and a collection of interesting steam engine models. He brought the tea pot, complete in his mother's hand-knitted cosy and bone china cups and saucers. There were even 'nice' biscuits to complete the picture.

Thinking back to the times at college when we had hysterically impersonated vicar tea parties, I carefully cocked my little finger outwards from the china cup and spoke in a pseudo-clergy voice. 'And how are we, vicar?' I asked, dramatically swinging my leg over to emphasise my listening mode.

Donald looked startled. 'Very well indeed, thank you,' he answered in a sort of 'auto pilot' voice. There was quiet for a moment, so he went on, 'And our new sermon series is going very well. I'm very pleased.'

'Your sermon series?' I answered in an equally startled tone. Was this the sum total of our old relationship, simply answering my silly question at face value and then talking about his latest sermons? Maybe he was acting his 'vicar tea party' response, I thought, and continued in that vein. But after a time I realised he was simply becoming the part we had once scornfully attacked. Where was the Donald I once knew? Where was the silly, gentle, thoughtful, caring mate I once laughed with?

Then I thought back to Josiah at the diocesan meeting. He was right. My friend had become a 'professional' religious expert rather than a real person. Nobody could have mistaken that he was the vicar, even if the dog collar he was wearing had been thrown to the four winds!

As we left, Mary, who had said little during the visit, remarked, 'Donald's in a real mess, you know. He put a face on it for you and me, but I just sensed he was really down. Didn't you?'

* * *

When God speaks he often brings bunches of things together to get our attention: Josiah, then Donald and then Greg . . .

I spotted 'Greg' across the college reunion room. Great, I thought, he would spark the day up a bit. My somewhat rotund friend was a real wit, 'Welsh and proud of it, boyo.'

'Hi, Greg,' I called to him at the first opportunity, and then sort of playfully punched his arm.

'Hello, Wallace,' he dutifully responded. 'Are you OK?' he

asked in a dull monotone that signified he didn't really want to know.

After I got over my 'is it me?' problem, I took him to one side and said, 'Come on, Greg. What's going on with you?'

After some very light bantering, Greg sat and told me about his disappointments. 'The churchwarden doesn't think people ought to laugh in church. And he has quite a following. "Ought to be more respectful," they say to me. But how can I? It's how I am.' He went on, 'And the church is losing ground, see, and they want it to be my fault. But they are such a load of old grannies. Always moaning. No wonder nobody wants to stay.'

'So what do you do?' I questioned.

'Well, I'm trying to be a faithful servant of the Lord in the place he's put me. That's all. But it's getting at me, see?'

Greg, Donald and Josiah's words preyed on my mind during the weeks that followed. Did people see me like that? Was I merely becoming a religious professional, weighed down with people's expectations and needing to get a life?

Mary and I had a habit, at that time, of sometimes going to a local Roman Catholic convent for a day's listening to God. The nuns were particularly helpful and always fussed round me, which I secretly liked. They insisted on calling me 'Father', which I found quite charming in that set-up.

Mary went off to a small sitting room to think and pray as I kept watch over the tea and biscuits. The nuns obviously thought, contrary to Mary, that I needed fattening up. We met up again for the three-course lunch that the nuns provided. Pity they didn't learn cookery as well as welcoming skills . . .

'Wallace?' Mary looked pleased. 'Do you know, God has given me these lovely pictures this morning. I was sitting and sort of drifting in the chair, and these images just started to form in my mind. I'm certain it was God,' stated my wife irrevocably.

I sipped my lumpy packet soup.

'I'm sure it was about people like your Greg and Donald, and what that man Josiah was saying as well. I saw a minister – don't ask me how I knew it was a minister – at the end of a long corridor . . .'

'Going to give me indigestion, this soup,' I helpfully commented.

'Listen, will you? In front of him hung curtain after curtain of horrible cobwebs. And he stood there, isolated and alone, like I said, at the end.'

'So what's this got to do with Donald and people?' I asked.

'I somehow knew the minister was in a real mess – unhappy and abandoned and things like that. Oh yes, and struggling with his faith. Then over it all, I saw a mask sliding down over his face. It simply said, "professional".'

'So what do you think all the cobwebs meant?' I asked after the nun had delivered the unappetising looking fish.

'They were a barrier, stopping the truth coming through. They acted as a separation – like a trap so the person stood separate. Do you see? You would have to sweep them all away to get to him.'

I vainly tried to scrape the black skin off the unknown type of fish. 'So how did you feel?'

'Compassionate. He seemed so lacking in hope and had become cynical. But the biggest thing was that he was living in fear. Fear of being exposed and being ridiculed and rejected. Just like your Donald, I suppose. So he had just put the professional mask over himself. Do you see?' she exclaimed with passion.

I stood up, feeling slightly repentant at having continued my lunch during Mary's explanation. I gave her a long fishy hug. 'I think your cobweb trap is exactly right. It's as if the devil is spinning his foul web to destroy ministers going forward in faith. And you're right. So many of us put on masks. I know I do myself for protection. And when does the mask end and the person begin? And is it just ministers? I've seen many Christians do the same: pretend that all is well and God is in his heaven, when really they feel like death warmed up.'

Mary ended, as the nun brought in the watery custard, 'It's the system as well. It's as if it can be used by the devil to spoil people's ministry – spinning religious stuff rather than developing a faith ministry in the living God.'

She turned out to be very right . . .

8
Putting a Face on It

> . . . that they will come to their senses and escape from the trap of the devil, who has taken them captive to do his will. (2 Timothy 2:26)

On a human level, you would have thought that God speaking to us like this would have brought joy and satisfaction and fulfilment. Mary's cobweb picture following on from my encounters with Donald and Greg should have pumped me full of wonder at God's grace in speaking to us.

My experience was exactly the opposite. In the days and weeks that followed it was as if I'd entered some sort of spiritual kick-back. And perhaps that was the truth of the matter.

Then there was the evening when I'd invited, unilaterally and without leadership or church 'ownership', a local church fellowship to join us for supper, sharing and prayer. It was a methodology of mission that I had been expounding at the diocesan renewal group, so I felt I had to put it into practice. Inevitably, relatively few of our people turned up. And those who did seemed disassociated from what was going on. Only afterwards did I realise I spent the entire evening making excuses to our guests, who clearly outnumbered our locals: 'I didn't really advertise this properly . . . I forgot that some of the house groups had specially invited guest speakers tonight . . . There's a PCC tomorrow night, so I expect folk had to stay with the family.' Anything to give the impression that I was a successful vicar with a church full of committed folk; that I was somebody to look up to.

I woke at 3:50 am the following morning with a sick headache – a disastrous time for me, especially when my mind switches to scan mode, looking for anything and everything to worry about. Having tossed and turned for about an hour I tuned my little headphone radio to the World Service and listened vaguely to something about a water project in deepest somewhere. Then I finally crept downstairs, stubbing my big toe in the darkness, resigned to a day of headachey tiredness. I thought to myself, 'At least the dogs will welcome me.'

And welcome me they did. Unfortunately, one of them had left a smelly 'parcel' ready for me to tread in with my already sore bare foot. I remembered how I'd unwisely fed them with some of the left-over church supper from last night. Not that I would tell Mary. She would just say, 'Well, you know curry goes straight through them,' with a look of 'it's your own silly fault' disdain.

Come ten o'clock I was ready to kill the chickens and shoot the budgie. Then there was a knock on the vicarage door. I knew it would be our flower lady, so I heaved a smile onto my face and became the ever popular vicar once again, as I went to inspect the new arrangements.

'Thank you, Blanche,' I said. 'Those lovely flowers remind us so much of God's creative power, don't you think? Bless you for spending your time making the church look so beautiful.'

Blanche yielded to my abject flattery and over-abundant praise, and smilingly retreated. I returned indoors to 'kick the dog' and skulk around looking for things to criticise.

'Now do you see what I mean?' questioned Mary later that day.

'Pardon me, but have I missed the plot?' I replied haughtily.

'What Josiah said about professional vicars. You've just proved the point.'

I had that dreadful feeling in the back of my mind that I was going to be in the wrong here, but bravely answered, 'What point would that be?'

'Last night and this morning. Both times. Last night you were running round like a scalded rabbit trying to justify yourself, and this morning you switched on your professional smile and spent half an hour being sickly sweet about flowers – which you're really totally uninterested in. Do you see what I mean?' she demanded once again in true Mary fashion. Nor was the monologue of my faults ended. 'Here you are telling me about Donald and Greg and criticising them for putting on a mask, and that's exactly what you do. What a hypocrite!'

'OK, OK,' I responded, putting my hand up.

It always takes me a couple of days to let things sink in, and it wasn't until we were quietly walking around Birmingham's botanical gardens that I was ready to think things through.

'I suppose that's what your cobweb picture means. It's as if I put a veneer on myself as a Christian: to church people and to the community – perhaps even to you and the family. A vicar mask, so that I keep it all at a slight distance. I didn't want the flower lady intruding into my personal space, so I became the vicar. Dead easy really.'

'Only it becomes "you" after a bit. Like Donald and Greg,' commented Mary as we stood together looking at the little stream in the oriental garden. 'It stems from a sort of fear really. Certainly not the fear of the Lord, but fear of being shown up as somehow less than a vicar should be and not the consistent, all-encompassing man of God you would like everybody to think you are. Do you see?'

'Yes. And to be truthful, I don't want people to know that I don't pray enough and have all sorts of lurid, cynical and unministerish thoughts. I want to keep people remote from my true spiritual position and somehow portray myself as a strong, able, spiritual leader.'

'And if you do that, don't you think that's true for everybody? It's simply human nature. But because you are a paid Christian leader, and on the front line, it's as if you've got something to prove. And the devil jumps on the back of it all, because it's a way in to destroy the church from the inside.'

Mary's prophecy started to spring to life. Could it be that the system of religion is throwing a cobweb trap over its ministers? That we have become too 'professional'? Not in the sense of doing our jobs right and well, but in the face we present to the world. And could it be that we get more and more drawn into this trap as the veneer becomes the reality, and the real us becomes more and more separated from the community?

For some ministers, the veneer of being a professional Christian has indeed become the reality. Gordon is a vicar in his mid-50s running a fair-sized parish organisation. He is not an outgoing man. Like many ministers he started as a sensitive, quiet soul looking to develop the kingdom of God within the limits of his own calling. But over his 20-odd years of ministry he has received many knock-backs, to a point where he is now known as 'that vicar who puts everybody's back up'. Like the time when he was publicly humiliated at an annual church meeting; dressed down by a well-spoken pillar of the community. Week after week he stands in the pulpit and senses that his preaching is inadequate. Some tell him so after the service.

One Sunday, Gordon had a very bad cold with a streaming nose, and inadvertently left his soiled hankie on the Lord's table. After the service, a 'Christian' lady of some years' standing said, 'Vicar, I thought it was quite disgusting to see your handkerchief on the altar. It is the Lord's table, you know.' Not a thought about his streaming cold and his battle to even come to the service that morning.

He looks at the church attendance figures and realises they are sliding, but what can he do? His frugal expenses are sardonically questioned at the church meeting. The church budget, once again, is failing. Well-meaning members ask him, 'When is something going to happen round here?' The choir group says, 'What we need is for you to get people into the choir.' The music group wails for 'more relevant worship', and the social committee wants to know why it is marginalised in the life of the church. The lady leading the cleaning group is angry because she cannot park on the vicarage driveway and says to him, 'Your trouble is that you don't care and you are driving people away from this church.'

Gordon sinks deeper into personal gloom and the mask gets more and more tight across his face. He survives, albeit without the faith dynamic of a few years ago. He is on the edge of a nervous breakdown, but he survives.

Slowly, things become stylised because any attempt to bring change suffers resistance and challenge. New ideas are met with: 'We've tried that before and it didn't work.' Gordon is careful to keep the liturgy precise; he keeps the church meetings formal; he ensures that his curate knows his place. He stops listening because he doesn't want to hear personal comments. He sits at his computer for much of the day. Nobody quite knows what he does, but he looks busy.

And slowly but surely the church sinks into a deadly rut. Gordon thinks, 'If only I could move on, get into somewhere decent. Then it would all work out.' He blames the parish, when the sad truth is that history will repeat itself in the new situation. The church has now degenerated into religion without power – legalistic ritual, which is the very antithesis of the Christian proclamation and the very situation that has allowed folk religion to grow to epidemic proportion in our nation.

Of course, full-blown 'Gordons' are relatively few and far between, although this characterisation has been built on my very real observations of friends and colleagues. Shockingly, some have not survived and have been broken by the process. Most ministers of all denominations can point to a Gordon somewhere in their past experience. Some have been a Gordon themselves.

The cobweb trap is spun by the devil. He loves to see the front-line soldiers of Jesus blown apart and will put any sort of 'spin' on committed discipleship to drive people away from the arms of Christ. That's his job in life (and death). The terrible web of deceit was spun round Jesus himself as he faced the severe temptations in the wilderness even before he started his ministry. His answers to the evil one bear repeating time and time again: 'It is written: "Man does not live on bread alone . . . Worship the Lord your God and serve him only . . . Do not put the Lord your God to the test."'[1]

Don't think for a moment this applies to leaders only. Gaynor had ceased to be a drug user through God's miraculous intervention in her prison cell. Drugs were a thing of the

[1] Luke 4:4, 8, 12.

past, but the consequences lived on in her family and even in Gaynor herself. She stood up at a local fellowship to give a testimony: 'Right there in the cell, I met with Jesus,' she shared from the podium. One could almost see the faith level rise in the engrossed congregation as Gaynor continued to expand her story.

'A real hero of faith, that woman,' said one broad black-country voice afterwards. 'Knows what she's talking about.'

Gaynor had finished with the classic 'Praise be to God', spoken peacefully and serenely, so that the world, or at the very least this small Brummie fellowship, was at her feet.

Of course what she said was totally true. But in her longing to proclaim Jesus' power, she had 'forgotten' to mention her personal rollercoaster of faith, that she was sorely missing quite a few parts of her old life and that ordinary church life was turning into a bit of a chore and a bore.

She didn't mean to put a face on it – it just happened. That was what was expected and she complied. The evil one was already casting his sticky web over her. Even Gaynor, the non-systemised new Christian, was beginning to fall into the devil's trap of wearing a mask and hiding truth, even from herself.

We as Christians are in the trenches of life. When Sabine Baring-Gould penned that great hymn 'Onward Christian Soldiers', she knew so clearly that being a Christian is both the finest and the hardest thing in this world. It's a battle as well as a triumph.

9

They Paint the Walls with Domestos

. . . neither are your ways my ways. (Isaiah 55:8)

Roland was in love: with life, with love and especially with Flick. As he checked the temperature of the big pottery kiln, his mind was engrossed with the young lady in the gift shop. There she would be, smiling as usual, as she sold the holiday souvenirs he had created that very week. They were a partnership, Flick and he, although as yet she didn't know it. But as Roland thought of her trim figure and golden hair, he knew they were destined to be together. But how was he to approach her? She was like a remote goddess to him. How could such a person be interested in a dowdy backroom potter?

His big moment came that evening, just before he was due to finish for the day. Flick smiled at him and started to chat. Then suddenly *she* was inviting him out! 'Roland, why don't you come along with me to church on Sunday night?' said his unreachable idol.

His heart started to beat wildly. He'd have followed her to the ends of the earth if she'd asked, but he simply muttered, 'OK' and then started to sort out the details.

Roland had never been to church before. He was not religious, so why bother? And the service was irrelevant to him.

What mattered was sitting next to Flick. That was brilliant. His sensitive nature was drawn by her innocence and simple joy in living.

'Like to come along to a rally on Wednesday?' questioned Flick.

What did 'rally' mean? Who cared? As long as they were together.

The preacher spoke directly to Roland. Or that's how it seemed to him. He was the only person there, he felt. Except for Flick, of course. In one part of his mind it was outrageous to respond to the invitation to go forward for prayer, yet another part felt a strange inner compulsion beyond his understanding. He felt in some astonishing sense that it was all bigger than even Flick herself.

He found himself in front of the preacher, who looked directly at him, placed his hands on his head and demanded, 'Receive the Holy Spirit.'

Roland hit the floor, Flick by his side. Wonderful.

I met Roland some years later. He had married his Flick and become an Anglican vicar. They were an unchurchy tender couple, full of love for Jesus, delighting in the Spirit of God. Roland's curacy had been successful, if uneventful, and his natural naivety had flourished. Their sense of calling to the deprived had led them first to a large estate in the inner city. He was an extraordinary and outstanding minister of the gospel.

'What shall I do?' was his first question to Mary and me. They were clearly in great distress over the religious and rigid ways of some in their new flock. 'They just sit up there, on the balcony, next to that huge organ, and when I preach, I know they don't listen or even pretend to listen. I can hear them talking and sometimes tittering. And so can everybody else. Not that there are many others anyway.'

Flick had lost that carefree bloom. She was worried about her beloved Roland and so frustrated at the choir, who, in her mind, were ruining everything. And she so wanted the little church to be full of Jesus.

'I asked Winifred if the choir could come down for the sermon,' said Roland, as if there had been a major confrontation. 'She just said, "That's the way we do it here. It's always been like this, and we like it this way."' He looked rueful and continued, 'so what else could I say?'

Flick put her arm round him tenderly.

Within two years, Flick and Roland had left the church and the Anglican ministry. I met them at a Christian do some time later. 'Did you make the right decision?' I asked them. Their situation had been a burden on my heart and I'd always felt I could have done more to help. They still had their arms around each other, and looked even more how a Christian couple should be.

'Absolutely,' they said as one. 'We didn't want a fight, and we certainly didn't want religion.'

'And Wallace,' Roland added, 'the Lord has been leading us into other areas of ministry, like pastoring people. That's what he wants us to do, and we don't have to battle with churchy people any more. We can be ourselves in Jesus.'

'Yes, that sounds good. And right for you.' How could I do anything but smile at this brilliant pair? But what a sad loss to the Anglican church, I concluded.

* * *

Leonard was another excellent minister.

'It's just too late,' he remarked in a forlorn voice. 'I've

turned sixty now, and what else can I do? I've got to see my years out.'

Mavis his wife nodded in despondent agreement. It was obviously a much talked about subject, and they were resigned to what they viewed as the inevitable, old before their time.

Mary and I had met the Millers some months before at a renewal conference. Leonard had been so enthusiastic about his faith and clearly enjoyed the renewed worship. Here was a good friendship possibility, so we exchanged addresses.

The directions to their rectory led us down an enchanting lane, deeply situated in the midst of an archetypal English village. The church was in a sort of wooded glade and one could glimpse the wooden beams of the picturesquely ramshackle entrance porch amid the manicured lawns and shady trees. Behind stood their graceful Queen Anne three-storey home. Its mellow stone elegance fitted the arcadian scene wonderfully. The whole combination of church and vicarage looked quite charming.

But a closer look belied the rustic idyll. Decaying doors hung askew on the outbuildings, tiles were missing and there was a depressing air of faded grandeur. There was peeling paintwork on the house and a once proud lawn was running to seed, with flowerbeds of nettles.

Mavis greeted us warmly and took us into a kitchen of glorious dimensions. But instead of being set out with complementary fitments and a wonderful Aga, it had rickety tables and old broken easy chairs. It smelled of mould and bleach.

'This is our warm room,' apologised our hostess as she made our cup of tea. Warm room? What did she mean? A rather harassed Leonard appeared halfway through our drink, and they took us on the grand tour.

The rectory was a remnant of grander days, when the vicar and squire were *the* people of the rural community. Leonard's study was an amazing room of gigantic proportions, but cold and clammy. There was a church council room, with a huge oak table stretching the full length, and a spacious and rather lovely staircase. As I peered nosily upwards I could see a huge sheet of heavy duty plastic closing off the third storey. We ended up in their 'stately home' lounge.

'I'm sorry about the damp and the smell,' Mavis remarked. 'It's the only way we can keep the mould down. We have to paint the walls with Domestos every few months.'

Leonard joined in, 'We can't afford to keep this place warm, let alone do any work on it.' He walked proprietorially over to the sash-type French window and said, 'We would like a proper rectory, but the brigadier likes his clergy here.' The brigadier?

As we retired to the warm room, the unhappy rector explained: 'We can't do renewal here. You see it's all down to the brigadier. He lives across the valley there. He's churchwarden and patron, and runs the village. He's got a personal helicopter and every year at the church fête he takes people up for a tour of the area. That's how our little church stays solvent – through him and his helicopter. And he's good to the church in other ways. If anything needs doing, he'll send a couple of men round.'

'But we can't do renewal,' Leonard repeated lamely. 'The brigadier doesn't have any time for "new-fangled stuff", as he calls it.'

Mavis took up the story. 'So we go out to conferences and sometimes to that Vineyard church in town. It's what we have to do. It's all we can do.'

Sadly, our friendship never progressed beyond that visit. Mary made the point clearly: 'I just didn't know how to handle it all. They really love the Lord – we know that – but what can they do? That brigadier holds the power and the purse strings, so that's it. And I began to feel almost guilty that our church is active and alive.'

'And what about that brigadier?' I responded with unfeeling gusto. 'I can almost imagine the old villagers touching their forelocks. I wonder if he still has his own pew? I bet he does.'

'Wallace, have a bit of thought for Leonard and Mavis, won't you? It's as if they are held in bondage. Think how desperate and helpless they must feel. But what can they do about it?'

'Get another job?' I answered dramatically.

'Don't you understand? It's as though they are victims. They have a real heart for their community and want to pull down all the old-fashioned churchy barriers so they can really welcome people in; make the church accessible to them. But the system has knocked them for six. They feel powerless and abandoned.'

* * *

I was once guest speaker at an evangelical free church. They were without a pastor for the fourth time in as many years, but excited about the new prospect, who had 'preached with a view' the previous Sunday.

'A man of the word, you see?' said Gideon.

'Straight down the line,' expressed Amos without so much as a smile.

'Thirty minutes without glancing at notes – a real preacher he is,' confirmed Gideon.

Mary looked on with a tiny amused smile as I furtively hid my notes and mentally resolved to be 'free in the Spirit'.

The tragedy of this comic opera was the pastors themselves. They were reduced to anger and frustration as they sought prophetic ways forward in an environment where the people really wanted to return to their successful 1960s heyday. I remember my later conversation with this 'man of the word', whom I saw as a very able young pastor . . .

'They want children in this church – or so they tell me!' Bryan was almost shouting with rage as he strode around his little church office. I could see he was ready to punch the walls in sheer frustration. 'And that's what I've done. There they are. Every Sunday. But now they want them to be quiet and sit still all the time; not to say a word to disrupt "their" worship. Have you ever heard of such a thing?'

I made some noises of assent. He wanted me to listen, not to be yet another voice telling him what to do.

'I just don't believe it. And now they've told me to go. "You don't fit into our ethos," they told me. Sitting like prize turkeys around a Christmas table, they were, smiling benevolently down at me and explaining about "true" worship.' Bryan slapped his hand down hard on the filing cabinet to accentuate his exasperation. 'And that's it. I've got to go. A year of my life wasted.'

Gideon and his fellow elders had a real burden to rebuild their once thriving church, but they could not leave the past behind and their ways had to be *the* way. The system of being church had taken the place of Jesus. The sadness was that

Gideon and his people were, in many ways, brilliant Christian people. What a shame and a waste.

* * *

These internal barriers, which can be set up unconsciously, by many churches became the topic of conversation as Mary and I sat down with our supper guests, Jock and Sheena – especially the little evangelical fellowship that seemed the most poignant, painful example . . .

'So many churches that really want to grow and thrive and tell people about Jesus get caught up in stupid systems,' I said.

Sheena and Jock were friends, so Mary and I felt a growing confidence to share our deeper thoughts with them.

'To me it's the same old story,' Sheena briskly commented. 'Churches just get stuck in a rut. It doesn't matter at all whether they're Anglican or whatever. It's the same old story. They need to sort themselves out!'

'Sheena, I agree with you. You're right. Take a second though to add to what you're saying,' I rejoined. 'They are what they are, because they are what they are.'

'Excuse me?'

'What I mean is that those congregations have developed in the way they have because there has been no sense of service, no sense of being there for others. So many have had their own needs pampered to rather than being challenged with the absolutes of the gospel. It's like Flick and Roland. The choir had got away with ungodly behaviour for far too many years, hadn't they? It had become normal. And Roland was just too much of a non-confrontational person to even begin to sort it out.'

'Yes, don't forget that many leaders are really sensitive people,' commented Mary. 'The last thing they can handle is confrontation of any sort. It's part of what they are and why they are there. It's like expecting Leonard to stand up to the brigadier. What a thought!'

It's the whole system that's cock-eyed,' stated Jock emphatically. 'I can't believe what you guys tell me of how it is on the inside. Amazing! I mean, where's the faith dynamic? It's not surprising the church is losing millions of people,' he overstated. 'And anyway, why do so many ministers even look like fluffy woollen cardigans? They're just going along with what always was, conforming to expectations, smiling benignly at everybody, chuntering platitudes . . .'

No half measures with this man, I thought.

'Who is the boss of you lot anyway? Is it the congregation or is it God? You baptise anything that moves, and you would say "there, there" to murderers given half the chance . . .'

'Jock, Jock,' I interrupted with a smile. 'I love your generalisations, even though you don't believe them yourself, but in a way you are spot on. Many churches have so lost the plot that they are merely in limbo to the modern world. You are so right to ask about the faith dynamic.'

'Seems to me the church needs to sort itself out before it sorts out the world,' stated Jock categorically.

It becomes clearer and clearer how rigid church ways, together with some powerful people wielding power to their own ends and even godly people who are unwilling to change, have held up the proclamation of the gospel. How important it is that we ponder and act on the astonishing faith dynamic of Jesus himself, who cut a gigantic swathe through the barriers of the religious system so that the kingdom could be announced.

However, God in his wisdom was preparing me to experience other barriers to faith. First the ultimately faith-destroying 'prosperity gospel', and beyond that the unseen power and distortion of folk religion . . .

10
A Single Red Rose

In this world you will have trouble. But take heart! I have overcome the world. (John 16:33)

Jane had been a 'gentleman's' masseuse, a nightclub hostess, a brothel keeper, a blue cinema manageress and a heroin abuser.[1] I say 'had' because her beautiful body, corrupted by its cancer, now lay in the sleek wooden casket at the front of the church.

I remembered how, years before, God had spoken to me of her inner needs even before we'd met: 'Wallace, I want you to tell Jane that I know her from the inside. I know she is devoid of any sentiment at the moment; that she feels hard and callous, even towards her children; that she is existing in a sort of time warp, separate even from herself; that, to her, life holds no value or answer, only a consuming bitterness.' God's voice in my head continued: 'You must tell Jane she is my child and she belongs to me; that I love her in spite of everything. Tell her that I am her heavenly Father.'

The previous day I'd had a surprise telephone call from her friend Maggie: 'Vicar . . . can you help my friend Jane?' And we'd quickly arranged the visit. I think it was the

---

[1] See *Angels on the Walls.*

urgency and the unknownness of the situation that forced me into prayer that morning. Of course, our God knows the end from the beginning, so he was waiting and ready to place the unexpected word of knowledge within me.

Over the next weeks and months and years, that word from the Lord bore abundant fruit as Jane totally rejected her former lifestyle with its gaudy type of adventure and materialistic excitement. She became a wonderful Christian woman, full of repentance for the past, yet vivaciously alive in Jesus. It had been visible to everyone that he was her Saviour and Lord and would remain so into eternity. Her four children slowly emerged from privation and abuse to making their own personal commitments. What a miracle for this modern-day Mary Magdalen and her offspring.

Yet here I was, about to conduct her funeral at the tender age of 34 years. For me, the vicar of three outer council estates, it was one of the worst moments of my life. There, at the front of the church, was the slim coffin that held the terrible reality of Jane's dead body. A few yards away her four children huddled together, wrapped round each other, sobbing piteously and emitting low wails of total anguish.

I felt a deep, underlying anger. 'God, why didn't you heal her? I don't really believe that this awful situation will work out for the best when I think of those poor children. It isn't enough to speak of eternity when the present is shattered.'

I glanced over at my wife. She was only inches away from the wailing children. Our eyes met for a moment; the shared past of ministering to Jane joining us together, yet the pain seared between us, forcing our gaze to drop. I could see that she too was in profound distress.

I looked around at the overflowing church. It was immediately clear that Christian victory over death was far from their corporate mind. They sat numb and silent, even though they had known for some time of the malignant melanoma, caused by constant use of a sun bed in her former life, consuming her body.

I allowed the familiar Christian words to come forth: 'I am the resurrection and the life . . .' and the congregation attempted to be Christianly joyful, knowing that Jane was with her Lord. But what about now? What about the children?

After the service Mary joined me in our car and we slowly followed the hearse to the cemetery. She remarked with a quiet passion, 'Jane will be with the Lord in glory now. She'll experience the truth of those angels from our walls those years back. Have you thought of that?' Mary was thinking out loud as we both tried to come to terms with our loss. 'I told her, you know, "Heaven will be so wonderful – beyond our imagining." Yet I can remember Jane saying, "How can that be so, without my children?" And we talked and talked. "Somehow God will work it out in his way, even if we don't understand how that can possibly be," I said to her.'

'But Wallace,' Mary continued, 'did you see how the children were sobbing their poor hearts out? Who on earth is going to look after them? It will be social services that end up legally sorting it, you know.' She looked at me with tears in her eyes: 'They won't let Biddy adopt the two little ones like she wants to. You'll see. And anyway, would it be right, splitting them up like that?' The questions trailed on and on and she wrung her handkerchief in total frustration. 'We're so helpless to do anything about it.'

The cars entered the cold cemetery and stopped near to the open hole in the dank earth. As I called the many folk together, so the coffin was lowered: 'Earth to earth, ashes to ashes and dust to dust.' The four shocked, traumatised and now silent children stood, each clutching their rose stem as if their life depended on it. Only the second child managed, belatedly, to throw her single red rose onto the wood six feet below.

As we journeyed home together, there seemed to be nothing to say. But later that evening as we sat by our open fire the feelings started to come to the surface.

'One thing I do know,' I commented cautiously after a time of quiet, pain-filled thoughts. 'Jane's funeral was so authentically Christian it almost made me weep. You know what I mean? It had spiritual depth and power, even through the pain. I mean, I know that she's with Jesus and that makes some sort of sense. But Mary, why did God choose to allow it to be this way?' I couldn't stop talking. 'Do you remember how he spoke to me supernaturally about Jane when she was still a "hostess", and then to her child in hospital? So why not speak to the cancer? If God is so all-powerful, why didn't he simply click his fingers and sweep it away? How can I deal with a God who seems arbitrary in his ways? How can I tell people to have faith? I don't know that I'll ever be the same person again. I feel so utterly disappointed with God. Does a faith ministry make sense any more – that's what I want to know?' My voice rose to a crescendo of anguish. 'I can understand now why people choose religion rather than faith. It's safer just to read the services, organise the church council and thank the tea ladies.'

After a moment I simply reiterated: 'Mary, I just feel so disappointed.'

* * *

We drove out to a restaurant the following night with Janet and Martin Knox. 'Do you remember how my brother was called to be a missionary in Kenya?' Martin commented.

After a slight 'hmmm' from his still emotionally exhausted guests in the back seat he continued, 'Then he was killed in a road accident. Can you believe it? Called by God, all the training to be a doctor and then killed in a road accident in the back of beyond. It just doesn't make sense, does it?'

We left the words in the air as we arrived at the restaurant and the waiter guided us over the tartan carpet to the corner table.

'Ah, real linen napkins,' I exclaimed as if it were important.

'My dad showed me the way through it,' continued Martin. 'He just kept going. He had faith enough to know that our Keith's death wasn't merely arbitrary. He never knew the reason this side of the grave, but remember how Dad went as a missionary speaker to Kenya – to the place where Keith died? Time and time again he went, even when he was eighty-odd. It was as if he had a compulsion to go there.'

Janet looked at her husband lovingly and I saw her hand slip into his across the table. It was as if the pain was still alive for Martin, and I think it was and is. These are no small matters.

Then Janet added her brilliant comment from her encyclopaedic knowledge of the Bible: 'At times we have to hang on to faith just like Shadrach, Meshach and Abednego. Remember what they said? "The God we serve is able to save us . . . but even if he does not . . ."'[2]

'I was just thinking,' said Mary, 'so often faith seems to

---

[2] Daniel 3:16f.

walk hand in hand with disappointment. Look at when Jesus cried over Jerusalem. Do you remember? "Jerusalem, Jerusalem, you who kill the prophets and stone those sent to you, how often I have longed to gather your children together . . ."'

Janet joined in, '". . . as a hen gathers her chicks under her wings, but you were not willing."[3] Yes, you're so right, Mary, Jesus did feel disappointment.' She went on, 'And how about when Jesus said, "Could you men not keep watch with me for one hour?"[4] He really showed disappointment in his disciples.'

'I daresay it's like I felt about Keith,' said Martin. 'That sense of disappointment. I don't pretend to understand, but somewhere it must make sense. That's where faith comes in. Not just accepting these disappointments, but believing that God is God and handing it all over to him.'

'And back to Jane,' I suggested. 'I still don't understand why God didn't just click his fingers, but I have to have faith that he's part of this, and that there is a reason.'

Mary added, 'It's the children that still pain me – snatched away from their mother and their friends and their church. I still don't know what will happen to them. But I suppose I have to give it over to God, like you said.'

Often things don't work out the way we would prescribe them. A loving couple make plans for a gracious retirement, then one falls tragically ill and everything falls apart. A baby dies in his mother's womb without even tasting the air of life. And violence ruins a person's life. Yet for the Christian, God is there in the midst, walking alongside and sometimes carrying us. What I fail to understand is how non-Christians

---

[3] Matthew 23:37.

[4] Matthew 26:40.

cope with the tragedies of life. Where do they turn to? What is their hope?

Christians do have to face up to disappointment. I get very angry with churches that suggest that showing disappointment says you lack faith. What nonsense! Churches that lay such guilt on their congregations are just as much in slavery to a system as the ones that offer institutionalised religion. It alienates people from God in not being allowed to show the true humanity of pain and suffering, and creates the false, unreal mask of happy religion, even when they are feeling like death warmed up inside. I came across one church where members were not allowed to grieve over the death of other church people because it showed lack of faith in the assurance of glory. Yet Jesus himself showed profound grief at the earthly loss of his friend Lazarus. Building an authentic faith means having to face fully and squarely up to the pain that real life can so often bring. It is little use pretending that all is well when clearly it isn't. If Jesus needed to cry, can his disciples expect anything less? It is the way of the cross; the way of Christianity in a broken and pain-filled world.

I for one have had my fill of the prosperity gospel. Health, wealth and happiness is not an earthly promise but a heavenly hope. Jane and Keith are in that eternal place where 'God will wipe away every tear from their eyes'[5] and all will make sense. The beauty of the front of the tapestry of life, which looks so confusing from the back, will spring to life for the Janes and Keiths and the unborn babies. That's the faith I have in a God who is bigger than all things and greater than the universe.

However, the wonderfully authentic funeral of a sincerely

---

[5] Revelation 7:17.

Christian woman did stir up many anxieties about the normal run of things and our system of dealing with death, and with its results on the spiritual understandings of our generation and beyond . . .

11

Grandma's a Star in the Sky Now

Man is destined to die once, and after that to face judgement. (Hebrews 9:27)

I carried the little container of ashes over the wasteland. In that cheap, plastic urn lay the physical remains of a young man. Alongside me walked his parents – good, honest working people. Following behind, the whispering retinue of mourners picked their way through puddles and rutted earth mounds, carefully avoiding the debris of unrecognisable iron litter and the occasional car tyre.

Suddenly Gloria slipped on a partly obscured mud slope. Instinctively I shot out a hand to steady her, and the jar containing the ashes of her only son wobbled precariously and almost emptied itself on the pathway. How is it possible for a human being to be contained in such a jar? What if it had spilt and his friends had inadvertently trod all over his physical remains? What had happened to Wayne himself? He was a man of little faith, as far as we knew, who chose to end his God-given life with suicide.

Ahead of us roared the motorbikes of Wayne's friends – a funeral farewell of track bikes marking the spot. As we arrived, and gently stepped over the remains of the police's red and white marker tape, I saw the branch over the dirty stream – the branch over which Wayne had thrown a rope, in great distress of heart and mind, and stepped out into the darkness of death. His girlfriend and children were nowhere to be seen. The recent and tragic break-up had been the catalyst of death by hanging.

In the past, suicides have been excluded from graveyards. Today we are more aware of the overwhelming pain, grief and susceptibilities of the bereaved. Also, society rightly allows us no such self-righteous judgements. But what have we Christians to say about death – suicide or natural? We clearly know what happens to committed Christians, but what about the others? Does the reciting of a Christian rite over their mortal remains give blessings? And if so, to whom? Or does it further propagate the folk religion that has now become a curse in that it invariably takes us away from the truth.

My curate asked me with a slightly worried smile, 'What I want to know is this: why isn't the world perfect?' Hilary had been shadowing me for quite a few funeral visits and was now branching out on her own. 'It should be, according to my visits. Rarely has anyone suggested that their beloved deceased is less than perfect. It stands to reason, then, that society must be perfect.'

Of course she knows her theology of original sin, but it is a curious fact that almost everybody seems to 'think well of the dead'. And that they have gone to 'a better place'. As ministers, we collude with this 'folk' acceptance of eternal destiny. After all, what other alternative is there? Can you imagine: 'Dearly beloved, I now commit your loved one to . . . hell'? I don't think so!

And as Hilary pointed out carefully and lovingly: 'It's not just us. All the Christians I know expect a good send-off for their deceased with all the promise of heaven, regardless of their faith in this life. It's as if we compromise all that we believe.'

I recall sitting passively at the back of church during a Christian funeral service for a relative whom I knew quite well. First of all, he self-confessedly was not a Christian, so unless there had been a death-bed conversion the service was a sham. However, the pastoral style of the minister was second to none. He clearly knew 'Fred' well, although he had never met him. For instance, I discovered Fred to be an accomplished yachtsman, when I knew for a fact that he would get seasick in a rowing boat on the local pond. His occasional difficult ways (of which there were many) became lovable little foibles. All in all, the minister gave the impression that here was a good man, worthy of heaven, with the literal words, 'a good life, well lived'.

It's easy to make fun of others, but I have often been in that position myself. The community's expectations that we should give the person a good send-off are immense, and all my training thrusts upon me a good pastoral style, regardless of truth.

In our churches and closed groups we talk about the unsaved; about judgement and hell. We chatter about the need for people to turn from their sins and accept Christ as Saviour. We eschew thoughts of normal, good people who are missing out on salvation. Some worry about spouses, relatives and friends who are outside the faith. We have a theology of abundant grace, interpreted in a million different ways but always focused on Jesus' saving death on the cross providing access to heaven for all who come to him. So what about 'them out there'?

Death produces amazing comments and smatterings of folk religion that bear little relationship to Christian belief:

'God wanted her to be an angel in heaven.'

'Heaven will be much better with Grannie in it.'

And the classic: 'She'll be a star in the sky, like Grandma.'

Or, 'He'll be OK up there with his wife/mother to look after him again.'

People would like me to say over the graveside, 'Now they'll be together again for ever. Nothing can separate them.' It's as if Jesus had never said, 'Those who are considered worthy of taking part . . . in the resurrection from the dead will neither marry nor be given in marriage.'[1]

Then, most common of all, there's: 'She'll be looking down on us right now and taking care of us.' As if death was truly 'the other side', separated only by a massive one-way glass window in the sky. I remember one person looking totally stunned when I logically suggested, 'But won't they be sad when they see your grief?' It was as though I had carelessly trespassed and spoiled a cherished comfort.

I remember one man plaintively saying to me, 'But it's God's job to love everybody. That's what he does. So of course she'll be in heaven!'

Of course, it's not up to us to judge. 'Neither do I condemn you,'[2] said Jesus to the woman caught in adultery. And it would be a terrible, ungodly situation for Christian people to make spiritual pronouncements on the person's soul and eternal lot. After all, didn't the thief on the cross next to Jesus repent at the last moment and Jesus promise, 'Today you will be with me in paradise'?[3] However, because of this 'heaven for all – regardless' attitude, we miss out on hell and judgement. It's simply not fashionable to mention such things, so Jesus' teaching is watered down.

---

[1] Luke 20:35.

[2] John 8:11.

[3] Luke 23:43.

Some weeks after Wayne's funeral this whole business was brought home in two very different, smoke-filled locations . . .

The estate pub was noisy and blue with smoke. I didn't really like it very much, but felt it was time to do some off-the-cuff evangelism in the local. Inevitably the subject got onto funerals because just that very week we'd had a very handsome pair of black horses draw a Victorian hearse up the road. I'd chosen to sit up front with the 'driver', which was an amazing experience.

'Well, nobody really knows what happens to people when they die, do they?' commented the man I'd struck up a conversation with in the pub.

'Not even you, vicar,' agreed his mate.

I considered this to be a terrific evangelistic opportunity and started to tell the story of Jesus rising from death to show us the truth of eternity.

But I'd immediately lost their attention. Their corporate mind was made up. Nobody knew, and that was the end of it. The subject was closed by common consent. Folk understanding and common acceptance that religion has nothing to say had struck again. And another intricately detailed, fully informed conversation about the merits of Aston Villa football club resumed. Now that was important!

I went on a funeral visit following an 'out of the blue' telephone call from the family of a parishioner who had just died.

'Come along in, man. It's good to see you.' The dominant family member welcomed me and shooed me into a crowded living room.

I noticed two things: everyone seemed to be smoking, and the television was on, showing a rerun of an old Benny Hill show, with Benny chasing near naked girls around an historic home. Funny how these details stay with you.

'It's OK,' said the same relative. 'The minister in yon hospital gave him the rites, you know. He was a lovely man.'

Who? The pastor or the father?

'He said to us, after Dad died, 'I'm sure your father is up in heaven now, after all the good things you've told me about what he was like. Somebody like him must be in heaven.'

His sister joined in happily, 'Oh, he was so lovely to us.'

My host spoke again, over the sound of the 'chase music', as I inwardly fought to keep my eyes and mind on the needs of the family. 'Now we'll be wanting you to take the funeral in your church. And we want you to give him a proper send-off.'

'Such a lovely man,' said his sibling in a repeat of earlier words. And Benny continued to chase the nubile girls.

Their corporate mind was made up. Their father was in heaven, the vicar had a job to do and that was that – sheer folk religion, ably helped by the hospital chaplain, or whoever he was. Nothing about salvation through faith by grace here.

* * *

The following week, after yet another Christian rite and 'Lovely service, vicar', I sadly went home for my post-funeral cup of tea. I turned to Mary and said, 'That's the system, you see. That's how it works.'

'Excuse me?' she questioned, not knowing my inward thoughts.

'It's the funeral I've just done. The family clearly told me when I visited them, "He wasn't religious, you know," yet there I was, mumbling the same words as I did for Jane – and everybody else for that matter. Am I just part of a system, churning out the stuff because that's how it is?' I went on, hardly pausing for breath, 'I really believe it's brilliant for people to have a godly funeral. We're made in his image, and that's good enough for me, but why the same words and same underlying assurance of heaven?' I slapped the table for emphasis, feeling really melancholic. 'You know, it so reminded me of your cobweb picture. I felt like a 'wheeled-on' professional clergyman, with robes and dog collar, spouting naive words of false hope. OK, I tried to preach the gospel, but it almost felt as if I was 'spinning' the great truths of heaven and hell to make a good funeral with kind and comfortable words.' I motioned at her with a tired shake of my head. 'Mary, I felt so lousy when people shook my hand afterwards. I'm sure I left about forty people saying "Nice funeral, vicar" and presuming I'd said that everything was fine and that he'd gone to a better place when, in reality, I'd no idea where that guy was at. Is it all just spin? Is that what God has called me to do?'

'Have you just realised that?' agreed Mary, when I was hoping she would be sympathetic and understanding. 'But it's not just you ministers, is it? All Christians have the same trouble. Remember Gail and her rat of a father? I know for a fact that for years he used to come back from the pub, beat up the mother and abuse Gail in all sorts of ways. If ever there was a cold, vile and vicious man he was it, and a million miles away from the faith. Yet Gail got you to do a real "faith" funeral – more for her and her peace of mind than anything to do with her father, I suspect.'

'But what choice did I have?' I put in.

'You pulled out all the stops just because Gail wanted everything to be all right. She wanted that cosy expectation of thinking the best, so she didn't have to face the uncertainty of not knowing the eternal realities for her father, and the burden of struggling with that. In her mind, even as a Christian, it was taboo to question the comforting folk truths.' Mary paused for a moment and then added accusingly, 'And you gave her what she wanted. I still don't know how you got the words out.'

'But Mary, can't you understand? It's just the way things are. It's as if I'm in slavery to a system of expectations that stops me from telling people what Christians really believe about death.'

I felt annoyed and boxed in by having to face the reality of the situation. And worse still, was I colluding with it all?

12
England Expects

Am I now trying to win the approval of men or of God? (Galatians 1:10)

I was watching the Harry Potter film when it came home to me. There he was, an innocent abroad, not understanding that he had power – power that could be used for good. As I sat alone in the darkened cinema, I thought, 'How often is the good the enemy of the best.' Jane's funeral, and the events following, had jolted me into thinking about the shallowness of what I normally do at funerals.

As young people ate huge cartons of popcorn in front of me and others hissed at each other and constantly changed seats in the midst of their youthful romance games, I mentally resolved not to come to a matinee ever again out of school term. But then Mary was away and as usual I felt a restlessness that forbade 'getting on with it'.

The film was OK, but vaguely boring, so my mind clattered around until it hit on Ruth and Jack. It was good that they were starting to talk about Ruth's illness, but was that the best? Would this Christian woman become yet another person to die in the best traditions of folk religion, or could we do something positive about things?

Ruth was recovering from an operation on a cancerous

growth in her stomach. She was a well-established Christian, yet I had the feeling that she was avoiding the surgeon's prognosis. As I had held Ruth's hands and prayed for her, it occurred to me that she was terribly frightened and feeling so lonely about the finality of her now terminal illness. There and then, in the cinema, in the midst of the rustling sweet papers and Harry Potter doing his amazing things, I decided that we would find the 'best' for Ruth; that she should not be allowed the mask of denial, nor forced into accepting folk religion traditions offered from her non-Christian family.

* * *

'We've got three months, so they say, before Ruth dies,' I told the staff team. 'Mind you, it could be tomorrow. That's my experience.' I then went on to share the hidden sense of fear I had perceived.

'She knows she's saved,' said my curate Hilary Savage. 'I've never met a person nearer to Jesus.'

Mary rejoined, 'But what does Ruth really know? So many people just revert to folk understandings and feel they can't ask questions because it somehow isn't quite English.' Mary sipped her coffee and continued with finality, 'What we must do is really teach her about heaven.'

Mary spent many hours with Ruth in the next months. Together they studied and thought and talked about death and judgement and heaven, as well as the actual process of dying. Gradually, as the Scriptures and the Spirit spoke to Ruth, Mary could see her eyes clearing of doubt and fear, even though her body was rapidly succumbing to the disease.

In particular Mary came home one afternoon really

excited. 'It was so good, Wallace. We were looking at that bit in John about the "many rooms"[1] and Ruth just propped herself up against the pillow and said with such a beautiful smile, "It's just so true, isn't it? My Jesus has a special place for me, ready and waiting. It's going to be all right you know."'

How amazing that Mary could bubble with joy after spending an afternoon with a woman who was dying. She went on, 'And Wallace, her eyes had that sort of far away, peaceful look – as if she could see it all for herself. I'll never forget that.'

Ruth herself said to me, 'You know, Wallace, you'll have to talk to the whole church about this.' She was still managing to come on a Sunday, but her frail body spoke of a very limited future on this earth. 'I want everybody to know, and I want to speak as well. I don't want it all hidden and glossed over. Do you see what I mean?' Her face showed an earnestness and power that was beyond argument.

As Ruth spoke later in church, tears formed in many eyes. The unspeakable was being shared, and the reality was beyond measure. Here was a woman of God who knew, as Jane did before her, that heaven's doors were open ready for her. Not because it's everybody's right, but because she had a Saviour who had died for her on the cross and saved her from her sins – the very heart of the gospel of Jesus Christ.

Of course, some said, 'Ruth shouldn't die. We must have more faith.' But death is a reality which can, and even must, be lovingly embraced by the Christian.

The funeral was outstanding. For the first time, that prayer, 'Save us, Lord, from dying unprepared' made absolute sense. The grieving at the earthly loss of a dear friend

[1] John 14:2.

was profound, but the sense of heaven's door being opened gloriously and completely so overwhelmed us all that it became a victory feast. And that's exactly how Ruth wanted it. '"Death has been swallowed up in victory . . . Where, O death, is your sting" . . . Thanks be to God! He gives us the victory through our Lord Jesus Christ.'[2]

The staff team spoke deeply about this event; we were all so moved.

'It seems to me that we have totally undervalued the process of dying,' said Hilary. Being an ex-midwife she was well used to hospitals and perceiving the priorities of patients.

'I have to say,' I concluded glumly, 'Ruth is the first person I've ever known to be properly and rightly prepared for death. We didn't even do it for Jane.' Then I looked up with a smile: 'You could see her spirit was actually soaring at the prospect of meeting her Jesus. It was wonderful.' I thought for a moment. 'But you're right about the undervaluing. The church takes so many funerals of people who have little or no faith, giving them a full Christian funeral, that when it comes to the real thing it's difficult to move beyond what we always do. We get so involved in doing good things that we forget the best.'

The staff team thinking on the issue was far from finished, as we discovered over the following weeks.

'But what can we do?' questioned my curate. 'Christian funerals for everybody who asks is what is expected of us. It's our job. It's what we do. That's the system. If we refused, it would be making judgements and would decimate the bereaved.'

'Not only that,' I returned. 'Free church and house church

---

[2] 1 Corinthians 15:54–57.

people expect it as well – of their relatives. And what about the money? Minister's fees help the Church of England to pay our stipends, and the church fees keep many churches solvent. We are stuck in a system that is impossible to break out of. But that's not the point,' I added. 'I'm completely committed to doing funerals for all who ask us. Everybody is created in the image of God and it's good that the church can offer a godly rite for every human being. My problem is that there is no distinction at the moment and that causes me difficulties.'

As I stopped to take a bite of my ginger snap, Mary broke in, 'It's even more complicated when you think about it. You see, folk religion has its good points as well. At least it keeps everybody looking to God in some ways, and even wanting a Christian funeral. And that can't be bad.'

I coughed as a crumb caught in my throat, so she went on: 'Anyway, Wallace, there is no way you can differentiate. You'll just have to keep on using the same words for wonderful Christians like Jane and Ruth, as well as all those others – like you were telling me about that wife-beater you did the other week.'

'It's true,' I responded. 'Look how I did the funeral for that guy who was really anti-religion. But his wife had said, "I want him put away properly, vicar." He'd roll over in his grave if he knew.'

Hilary chimed back in with a smile, 'Tomorrow the funeral director will ring, and I'll find it's to book a service for the local paedophile.'

The telephone rang as if to prove her point.

* * *

I feel myself stuck between a rock and a hard place. Because for so many years we have allowed the 'Englishness' of folk religion to grow unquestioned, it has all come home to roost. There are good and helpful aspects for our secular nation to at least acknowledge God at the point of death, but there's no excuse for allowing convention to drive our ways. It is surely more than time to firmly educate the church family and the community about the things of death. The worst thing is to allow the status quo to reign because it's easy and comforting. False comfort is no comfort at all, but something the father of all lies would rejoice in.

It's not just funerals that colour the folk religion of this country with the church's collusion. A brilliant Christian couple called Linette and Russ came to talk to me about their dilemma . . .

'Linette's sister has asked us to be godparents,' explained Russ, a wise Christian of many years' standing. 'And we don't know what to do.'

Linette piped in, 'You see, Wallace, our Melody is an agnostic – even dabbles in New Age stuff.' Linette obviously cared very much about her sister from the way she spoke her name. And it was equally obvious that she was delighted to be asked.

Russ continued, 'The family see us as the religious ones, so we were the obvious choice. And to be honest, I'm really blessed by the idea of being little Troy's godfather.'

'Trouble is,' Linette took up the tale, 'It's a full christening, and we'll have to stand with Melody as she and her partner say, "I turn to Christ" and so on. And to be honest, she hasn't. She'd be the first to admit it.'

'It's as if they are telling lies to God, and we are colluding with them,' spoke Russ with increasing anguish. 'What on earth can we do about it?'

'One thing's for sure,' pronounced Linette, 'I wouldn't miss it for the world. You know how much I love my little nephew. And I really do want to pray for him and be his godmother.'

'I'm with Linette,' returned her husband, 'but we've always scorned infant baptism for non-believers. Wallace, it's like we're going back on our faith. What on earth can we do?'

Russ and Linette became godparents for their nephew Troy. There was no other way to bless him and retain their relationship with Melody and her partner. As Russ said to me later, 'It's the way things are. We were caught up in the system. What choice did we have?'

Baptism is a wonderful command and sacrament – in the right place . . .

13

Made in the Image of God

The promise is for you and your children. (Acts 2:39)

The new village rector had learned all about christening and churchianity hoops, but never in a rural setting before.

'Rector, I've come for you to sort out the christening of little Dane,' said Alice, the village mum, with certain confidence. 'I'd like him done on Sunday the 29th at that three o'clock service. Just like my others.' She sat back with a smile. It would be a lovely family/village affair, with the rector doing his bit. Alice looked homely and satisfied, exuding that air of cakes already cooked and christening robe freshly ironed.

Vince had been waiting for this moment – with trepidation and worry. He'd heard on the grapevine that one of the 'old villagers' was coming, and here was the moment.

He coughed vaguely. 'I'm not quite sure we can do that date,' he replied with eyes cast down.

Truth is, the new rector wanted to be the new broom. In his first years as a church leader, he'd performed so many christenings where the sacred words 'I turn to Christ' had been a meaningless religious phrase before the sprinkling of the water. And in his last city parish he'd made some inroads into stopping infant baptism where it was clearly just a social gesture, an English birth rite, where the parent/s and godparents parroted the amazingly powerful words of promise to God. But it was only 'some' inroads, he would have been the first to admit. At least they had to attend his course and come to church a few times (was he to tick them off on a register?) and the christenings all happened at the main morning service – in theory anyway, unless the parent/s kicked up a fuss.

Vince fiddled tensely with his pen as Alice waited expectantly. 'You see,' he went on nervously, 'Nowadays we do what is called a thanksgiving service . . .' He paused for a moment and flicked his eyes up to her and then across to the two older ladies. 'Or if you really want a baptism we have to do a little teaching about it, and hold it in the main service.'

'First I've heard about that, rector.' The smile was not so broad. Alice too had heard rumours about the new rector and his ways, and that's why she had brought reinforcements.

Grandmother spoke up plaintively, 'Been our church here for donkey's years it has. My mother, her mother, my lasses' kids; all of us been done here.' She ended with, what seemed to her and her daughter, the total affirmation: 'It's our church, you see. Always has been.'

The other elderly companion nodded briskly with an 'I'll take no nonsense from you' superior smile.

'Well, you see,' went on Vince, 'it's the promises. You have to say "I turn to Christ" and "I repent of my sins" and so on. And your family never come to church. So-oooo,' he ended on a note of wariness. As well he might.

'Rector, are you saying I'm not a good Christian? Are you saying my family doesn't know all about sin? Are you saying we're not good enough? Is that what you're saying?' Alice demanded as she got nearer and nearer.

If Vince had been in a better moment, he would have enjoyed the double meaning of her family knowing all about sin, but he was frankly overwhelmed. He'd been taught to be nice and not confrontational, and it was just too much. 'Yes, I suppose you're right. The 29th did you say?'

Alice and her mother joined in the smile.

* * *

I believe infant baptism is absolutely valid for babies of committed parents. And I can also see why some Christian parents choose dedication. It seems to me that the Bible speaks both ways on this subject and, like many Christian truths, the answer lies in the paradox. God is bigger than the question.

But infant baptism outside of faith parenting I consider to be outrageous, even though I admit that God is still God and can work through our faults with his abundant grace. I well remember a discussion with a theological student who was spending a few months on placement with us in Birmingham.

'I can't believe vicars let this happen,' said the earnest young man as if there were no question whatsoever. 'How can you stand there and encourage people to tell lies to God?' He almost began to shout. '"I turn to Christ" indeed! What a joke. It's almost as if you lot are encouraging people into religious lip service so that they can get the baby done and have the party.'

'Whoooo, hold on a minute,' I put my palm up towards him. 'Think this through for a moment, will you, rather than just going off at the deep end?'

I told him the story about Vince.

'So what would you have done in his position? You've got

five village churches and a whole history, centuries of christenings. The previous rector christened anything that moved; he felt it was a sacrament and a right action of a faithful church, signalling God's love for all, without question. He was simply obeying the command of Christ to baptise all people in the name of the Father, Son and Holy Spirit. Well?' I looked quizzically. 'What would you have done, Bradley?'

He was slightly subdued. 'It's still not right,' he sulked. 'You can't make it truth just because it's always been like that. Anyway, I heard that in the olden days the Prayer Book talked about baptising through the faith of the church. But today's service doesn't say that, does it? It lays the onus on the parents. Isn't that right?'

'Bradley, think about it. Is infant baptism a blessing for the children through God's grace? Remember that Jesus said, "Let the little children come to me." Or is it a response to personal faith? What do you believe? Now that old village rector would have thought that God blesses children regardless, despite us.'

Bradley looked slightly strangled. 'But . . . but . . .' he repeated himself, 'it's just propagating folk religion, don't you think?'

I smiled in agreement. 'I think probably it is. But it does have repercussions in a society where the church has advocated for centuries that things be done this way.'

Bradley was not to be put off. 'But society is different now, isn't it? Not everyone is church connected any more. It's different now,' he repeated.

In reality, I thought Vince was wrong and Bradley had the truth of it, but I had to teach him and make the point, so I continued, 'But what about Vince alienating the whole village? Is that right? And then his future ministry will be blocked within that tight community. That being the case he might as well leave, because they simply won't accept him.'

Bradley looked at me with the earnestness of youth. 'Yeah, I can see it's a problem. But how can I be a minister if the system is going to prevent me from doing what I think is true? Answer me that.'

Later that afternoon, Bradley did his first 'behind the scenes' funeral. He stood beside me as we 'dispatched' an old soldier to the hereafter with pomp and flag and trumpet. The curtains at the chapel swished shut to the sound of 'Abide with me', and the mourners left.

'First one then?' questioned the crematorium supervisor. Even our young dynamic would-be vicar looked overwhelmed. 'Want to see out back then?' the man continued. Bradley smiled bravely.

The old soldier's coffin was slid reverently through the big iron door into where the gas jets awaited. The door was carefully closed and the attendant pushed the red button, igniting the flame. After short minutes the cremation was complete, but Bradley lingered.

'Is that it?' he commented in question form. 'A man dies and his body is burnt?'

'More than that,' I replied. 'That old soldier was from our local old people's home. The matron called me in just as he was dying, and I held his hands as we prayed. I guess the Romans would call it the last rites. He repented of his sins and made a commitment to Jesus – although the only church he ever knew was Sunday parade with the chaplain.

'Bradley,' I went on, 'there is so much more to birth and baptisms and death and all the rites of passage for us human beings. We are made in God's image; we have a soul. Now I get really messed up about how we do things and how much people take God for granted, but this I do know: that old soldier is loved by Jesus. Just as Alice is . . . and her difficult grandmother. So it's not all black and white, is it?'

* * *

Mary prepared the dinner: chicken with white wine sauce and a nice glass, or more, of Hock. As I loaded the dishwasher, Mary started to show Bradley the family photographs of our granddaughter. 'And that's at the baptism,' she carelessly commented.

'Baptism?' questioned my intense new friend.

'We're really pleased that our Elizabeth and Tim have chosen baptism for our Tabitha. I loved the way they waited until she was one, so they could really think through what God was saying to them. I think that's lovely.' Of course, Mary would anyway. Anything to do with Tabitha is 'lovely'.

'But people off the street. People who, as far as you know, have nothing to do with faith or God. What do you think then?' Bradley would not be put off as I listened in.

'Easy,' Mary answered. 'When they come to see us about things, we don't make a judgement. How can we? We've no idea about them. So we simply offer them an option.'

'How do you mean?' he answered, taking my proffered coffee.

'First of all, Wallace is really welcoming to everyone,' said my wife. 'He says how pleased he is that they have come along for their baby.'

I added as I sat down, 'Then I offer them the options, starting with a thanksgiving service. I tell them that it's a special service to do three things. First, to thank God for their baby and to celebrate his birth with family and friends

– it makes a special occasion. Secondly, it's a naming ceremony, so I ask what name they want to give for the child and then anoint him with oil as I prayerfully give him that name.'

'That's sounds OK to me,' said Bradley.

'And thirdly,' I went on, 'I encourage sponsors to stand prayerfully with us as I ask for God's blessing on the infant. Often, I'll give them a candle and ask them to set it on the family table at the "do" afterwards. Then there are things like certificates and so on. The thing is, Bradley, it's not about faith questions. I just love to have them standing up in God's house to seek a blessing for their baby. Can't be bad, can it?'

Bradley responded happily, 'Now that seems to fit in with what Jesus said about letting the little children come to him.'

Mary smiled. 'And we talk about Sunday school and church and things like that, and sometimes they will come along as a follow up – of their own free will. But what Wallace really likes is ringing the church bell.' Her eyes twinkled. 'I think it's all those Sunday afternoon naps he can disturb!'

The dogs followed us hopefully into the living room, always with an eye to any post-dinner snacks that might come their way.

'It gets them acknowledging God, and even maybe praying for their baby.' Mary looked pleased. 'Without lies, you see? Then Wallace tells them all about the infant baptism option. What that means.'

'So what about if they go for the baptism?' Bradley queried.

'No problem,' I said. 'We simply explain the promises they have to make to God as part of the service and ask them something like, "Are you ready to start bringing your children along to church yet?" and "Are you ready to make these faith promises to God?" Most times, people are honest about this and say, "No, it's not really where we are at at the moment."'

'What if they don't?' Bradley persisted.

'Like I said, they would have to go through the whole infant baptism package. You know, church attendance and a baptism course *before* we fix a date. At the end of the day, it's down to their own integrity. But, Bradley, there is no way I will encourage people to tell lies to God.'

Mary added, 'Most people are really pleased about the thanksgiving service, and word gets round, you know. So it's never come to a conflict yet.'

'And if it did?' questioned the dogged young man.

'I guess we'd have to pray for God's way forward,' I answered simply.

However, he would not be stopped. 'But what about in that village? What about your friend Vince?' he pressed.

'I don't know,' I answered feebly. 'I've never ministered in a village like that. But it must be possible not just to allow the system to dominate. I personally think Vince was wrong not to confront, but then I'm not Vince, am I?'

However, Bradley had the last word with the forthright candour of the young: 'Well, you lot are full of the right words, but I'm not sure.'

Of course he was right. But then people are so complex, aren't they? How can we govern the spirituality of Alice and the old soldier and the million and one untaught folk who just want what they want?

Bradley was also right in saying, 'I can't believe that vicars let this happen,' as he saw the poverty of our earthly response to God's grace. The church is all too often caught up in being nice to everyone and allowing its religious practices and ways to be swayed by the 'soft love' option. And the evil one enshrouds us with his sinister cobweb.

Yet I delight in a church that proclaims loudly that all people are made in the image of God and that God loves to touch their lives even though they might only come to him for 'hatch, match and dispatch'. Further, if we can bring some sort of Christian rite to their often godless existence I believe God will be delighted. Whatever else, we have the wonderful opportunity to proclaim the 'godness' of God, and the possibility of moving people on into a real faith dynamic – away from the religious establishment stuff.

I refuse to despise, as some would, the rites of the church. They most certainly are flawed by folk religion and in need of reassessment and restructure. But they give us a wonderful opportunity to minister God's grace into an increasingly secular and godless society.

14

Walking on the Moon

> Your young men will see visions, your old men will dream dreams. (Acts 2:17)

It felt as though the monumental, institutional iron gates marked 'religion' were swinging to behind me. I was nearly inside, nearly trapped. They reminded me sharply of that huge oak door of the vast, dark church of my childhood and the prison bars of my first brush with the ways of religious practice at my training church.

It had been gradually dawning on me as I talked with Bradley, the eager young trainee minister, that I was, in many ways, defending the status quo and justifying 'religion'. I'd done nearly a quarter of a century of institutional funerals, colluding with and perhaps helping develop folk religion; playing the game of church because that's how it was. Was I so unlike the battered archdeacon and the near-smothered men, Donald and Greg? Sadly I'd witnessed Roland leaving the ministry, but at least he'd not caved in to the pressures and had stood true to his faith.

As I went off to the Priory for a few days away, I felt sad and down-hearted. I felt like yet another toiling, 'professional' religious practitioner caught up with things rather than swimming freely in the power and anointing of

Almighty God. Mary's cobweb trap menaced my thinking. Was I too putting a mask on a routine, forlorn ministry?

I arrived as the monks were doing their midday prayers. They all looked so serene and godly in contrast to my down-heartedness and gloom.

Afterwards the head guy asked, 'Would you like some spiritual direction today?'

'No, I'd like to seek God quietly in peace, by myself,' I truthfully answered with some sort of composed gesture, and settled down to battle with myself in a seemingly vain attempt to hear God.

It's so good that God doesn't judge us according to our failings, because that night, in the Priory's little grey-painted bedroom, God laid an amazing dream into my heart.

In my God dream, I was walking along what I perceived to be the road of life, when I came to a crossroads. There were two possible routes to follow. To the left lay a beautiful, verdant landscape. It was safe and easy. Straight ahead was a bleak, barren and lifeless moonscape. I somehow knew this was to be my pathway if I were to follow Jesus.

I started forward, then suddenly realised I was clad in a spacesuit. Of course, it was totally logical in the dream. How else would I survive in that alien environment? Yet the effect of the spacesuit was to produce an aloneness and isolation. In the midst of these strange feelings, however, there was a stunning and amazing sense of the presence of Jesus. I realised I was striding purposefully with him on the moonscape.

After my few days away, I returned home ready for the Monday get-together Mary and I share with Martin and Janet.

'Here we are: coffee for Mary, tea for Martin and dream potent for Wallace,' Janet smiled as she set the drinks in front of us.

'You're showing your age, aren't you, dreaming dreams?' Martin dryly remarked. 'How old are you anyway?'

'Martin,' I said, ignoring my friend's banter and continuing as if the comment hadn't been made, 'there is no way this was an ordinary dream. It was powerful and God-given. Believe me, I've never been more sure of anything in my life. God was speaking to me.' I hesitated. 'I can see the edges of meaning, but what do you think?'

Martin went off to collect their children from the various activities of childhood and youth, while Janet and Mary talked about children and all sorts of personal things. I just sat and tried to think it through in a blank sort of way.

When Martin returned he said straight away, 'I know what all this is about. You're going to present "The Hidden Poor"[1] to all the outer estate vicars next week, aren't you? You'll see how they'll receive it. Nobody will agree with it, because they'll all feel so threatened. They will be really up tight and try to put you down because of what the report says. It will make them feel they have personally failed. You see if I'm not right.' Martin continued, looking me full in the face, 'You certainly will be isolated and alone. Make no mistake about it. But God is saying this is what he wants you to do. You see, it's a prophetic thing and you'll surely need the protection of that spacesuit. Does that make sense to you?'

Mary added, before I had a chance to reply, 'This is why you have been feeling so messed up lately. It's not that you are in the wrong, it's simply that God is sharpening up your thinking so you are ready.'

Martin agreed. 'And I bet it doesn't stop there. You will

---

[1] Wallace and Mary Brown, with Martin and Janet Knox, 'The Hidden Poor' (Birmingham Diocesan Survey of Outer Estate Churches).

have to speak at so many places about kicking the system. Believe me, you will feel so alone at times, it will be scary.'

God is good. A few days later, as is the way of God, an encouragement arrived through our letter-box. Mary Chamberlain had written from Norwich, with absolutely no knowledge of my dream, telling of a word from the Lord about me standing in the middle of a barren moonscape in a spacesuit. Amazing! If I needed God's confirmation of his calling on my life, this was it.

* * *

The meeting wasn't going well. I'd just presented the 'Hidden Poor' paper to the ministers from the outer council estates. Mary and I, together with Martin and Janet Knox, had spent quite some time compiling the statistics and conclusions about the dire state of these churches.

'Crisis? What do you mean crisis? Don't you think that's a bit of an emotive word?' said one of the vicars.

In truth I was getting heated. I was presenting the appalling statistics about church attendance on the estates: 'Look at the report. It shows that the average estate congregation is a mere thirty-five people, and they are mostly elderly and not part of the estate culture. And look at how few children there are.' I continued strongly, 'All of us are heavily subsidised by the rest of the churches in our diocese. Did you know that?'

What the ministers did know was that they were feeling uneasy, as if, somehow, I was attacking them and saying it was their fault, just as Martin had predicted. In truth I was merely pointing out the statistics of the failing council estate churches. We were all in it together. As I pointed out, 'The Anglican church does not work very well on the estates.' In fact, as I was to discover, few churches of any denomination work well within the estate culture. The bad news had to be accepted before change could be brought about, or even considered necessary.

'And look at how many vicars are leaving the estates. Did you know that, at this very moment, four vicars from the estates are having some sort of breakdown? And surely you've heard about the dreadful fireball between that estate church and vicarage just a few weeks ago caused by those so-called joyriders torching the car?' I ended up with the plea, 'Come on, you guys. Just be real about these things!'

'Couldn't you have picked a better word than "crisis"?' retorted my wary antagonist pressing home his point. 'It's just too emotive.'

'Well, what about the emotion that Tony's suffering?' I almost shouted back, forgetting confidentiality in the heat of the moment. 'He's given twenty-odd years to the estates and all he gets is abuse from the neighbourhood and fewer and fewer people coming to his mass. Wouldn't you call that a crisis?'

With that my opponent rose to his feet. 'I thought this was a business meeting,' he shouted, 'not some sort of evangelical clap trap.'

'But don't you see?' I retorted purposefully. 'It's not even just about us Anglican clergy. I was leading a nationwide group of Baptist ministers the other week, and they are having exactly the same sorts of issues. Did you know they are closing the church down on that estate near your place because of vandalism and low attendance?' I ended forcefully as he stood over me, 'Don't you think that's a crisis? Or do you think the whole Baptist Union are just being emotional?'

It was just too much for my 'friend'. 'I'm going,' he shouted. And with that he stomped across the room with a total lack of grace, and threw the door violently shut behind him.

I felt awful. What had I brought about? Yet the report needed to be written and the problems seen and accepted for what they were. And I clearly knew God was with me. This was my lonely trail: to speak prophetically into the system and to precipitate change for the better in his church. This was a direct outworking of the moonscape dream. I also knew that in many places other people were doing similar things, and that together we could help bring about God's purposes.

Amazingly, and this must have been God, a few meetings later and after much individual work with selected leaders, the report was warmly accepted and has since formed the basis of our outer estates policy in Birmingham. Furthermore, Mary and I were able to lead a nationwide group of seminars to all denominations through the Church Pastoral Aid Society, speaking on the same document. My moonscape experience led us to places as far apart as Belfast, Dundee and Portsmouth. Isn't God amazing when we take the bull by the horns and follow his ways?

All of us Christians are called, in this sense, to be prophetic. The 'broad path' in the verdant pastures always beckons becomingly. For some, the religious life is like that: safe, secure and green. Within the boundaries of Wells Cathedral there is an archetypal English road of houses called Vicar's Close. All is safe there. It is the ultimate in security – or so it seems – and part of me longs to live and breathe in such a place, with money, position, status and power. The images of this world are so masterful to our fallen nature.

Yet Jesus commands every one of us to seek out the narrow gate and follow the narrow way 'that leads to life'[2] – the barren moonscape where we only exist through the empowering of the Holy Spirit. As Martin would later so truly remark, 'All Christian people are called to be prophetic; to speak out against the sins and wrongs of this society and to follow the Master through Gethsemane and to Calvary.'

Jesus, I slowly remembered, stood up in isolation against the religious system of his day. So much is said about Pharisees and scribes in the gospel . . .

---

[2] Matthew 7:14.

15

Mountains and Mustard Seeds

> I tell you the truth, if you have faith as small as a mustard seed, you can say to this mountain, 'move from here to there' and it will move. Nothing will be impossible for you. (Matthew 17:20)

I backed my Citroen Berlingo carefully down the sharp concrete ramp onto the Caledonian McBrane ferry, *Eilean Egge*, for the short trip from Oban to the Scottish island of Lismore.

As the ferry crossed the Lynn of Lorn to berth at the tiny terminal of Achnacroish, the stately Oban Cathedral lay to the right and the misty hills of Mull to the left. The two cars and straggly half-a-dozen passengers left the red boat to negotiate the single track backbone road of the island. Mary and I arrived at our wonderful ex-limeburner's cottage in the village of Port Ramsay as the late afternoon sun reflected across the still waters of Loch Linnhe. It was beautiful beyond words.

On the Sunday morning we drove the short distance to the island's only kirk, to receive a warm welcome from the large proportion of islanders who still attend. At the stroke of 12.30 pm, out of the little room at the back, appeared the six elders (looking suitably Scottish and traditional) followed by the minister, and the service began, following the order of centuries and the system of the Church of Scotland. Indeed, the parish magazine told of the 1806 Communion token 'which is still used in Lismore Church'.

Every church has its system. People know roughly what is going to happen most Sundays at St Boniface as we are part of the Anglican communion and subject to its bishops and ways. If I go into a free church, I can predict with fair accuracy how the service will progress, as well as the background system of governance. Visits to the new churches give me the anticipation of more than 30 minutes of fairly stylised modern worship, followed by a similar length of talk and then, maybe, some sort of ministry. That's the way it is. We all need our systems and methods of being church. The problem comes when the system becomes bigger than the message. Or even when the system becomes the message!

I walked along the unmetalled track towards the Lismore lighthouse. Charm, our golden Labrador, ran alongside me, eying up the watchful sheep as they stood on rocky crevices. The loch stood silently still to my right, yet pitted with the soft rain that was steadily soaking my cagoule.

Yet we need a system, I thought to myself. Systems tend to be self-serving, but we need a system.

Mentally I looked back at the Old Testament, scriptures full of stories of how systems were set up to enhance the work of the kingdom. I thought of Moses delegating his work to the many elders and Ezra ordering the temple worship. Trouble was, the system always seemed to become greater than its objective. The system of temple worship tended to eclipse the spiritual reality.

The pathway ended at a muddy farm cottage and outbuildings that had clearly been abandoned some years earlier. The old door lay askew on its rusted hinges, so I went in. The antiquated cast-iron stove, complete with oven and skillet, stood proudly in its red rust. In the corner was a chocolate-painted door leading to a bedroom, with its 1950s wallpaper damply intact on the bumpy walls. Charm was more interested in the sheep droppings.

I cogitated as I mounted the hill towards the Lighthouse island. Religious systems always seemed to tend towards corruption, just like people themselves. Original sin, I supposed. And by the time of Jesus, the scribes and Pharisees had totally lost the plot. The system was so developed that it could not be sacrificed even for the Son of God.

The rain continued relentlessly as the lighthouse came into view. Amazing! A ship was carefully negotiating the Sound of Mull in the background.

I leaned against the sheep fence at the end of the island and continued to chew it all over. But hang on a second, I thought. Even Jesus set up an embryonic system as he called out the twelve disciples as leaders of 'the way'; and he even had Judas as the first treasurer! So that must mean that it's not the system that's wrong. It's needed to express the reality of the faith community and to protect the treasure of good Christian teaching and ways. There wouldn't even be a Bible if we hadn't had some sort of system.

On the way back, my dog took it in her mind to chase a herd of bullocks. I yelled at her as she danced around the beasts, and I was very pleased there wasn't a farmer in sight.

I remembered a similar walk around Tilgate Park in Crawley, the home of my eldest son, Jeremy, who had become a children's worker at St Mary's.

I'd been thinking then about the system of the church that has led to so many problems over the years; necessary yet impossible systems that have grown greater and greater so that today we see places like the Vatican, which seeks to espouse simple faith but is also a multimillion-pound organisation.

As I walked, an image came to my mind, which I shared with Mary and Jeremy afterwards as we sat down to our evening supper from Jeremy's local take away.

* * *

I helped myself to a more than adequate portion of beef in black bean sauce. 'I had this image come to my mind this afternoon,' I told them. 'Strange it was – like a mountain of dough.'

Jeremy looked at me in the pitying way that sons look at their aged fathers. 'Dough?' he repeated. 'Like bread dough, do you mean?'

'Yes,' I plunged on. 'To me it was a symbol of the church system. Whenever I tried to move it, my hand just sank into the dough, made a fist-shaped mark for a short time and then the whole thing just quietly and completely returned to its original shape. Or nearly, anyway.' I began to feel excited about my revelation. 'Do you see?' I exclaimed.

The blank faces told me everything.

'You know that we need to do something about the church. It doesn't hit the mark at the moment – everybody knows that. Look at the attendance figures. And whenever we try to reform the system, there is a short-term reaction and we think "yessss!" and then slowly and inexorably it seems to return to where it was originally, as if the work had no effect.'

I greedily helped myself to more of the duck in orange sauce, together with a fistful of prawn crackers.

'You see, people put amazing energy into faith ventures. Things change for a while and then seem to return back into the system and they feel so disappointed – it's as if their work was to no avail. The whole thing just seems to roll, duck and dive, absorb the energy and return to the status quo. But it doesn't really. There is always movement, even if it's not plainly visible. Do you see what I mean now?'

'Yes,' Jeremy tapped the table. 'Are you thinking of things like Toronto and Pensacola? It seems as if they have come and gone and that's it. But what you're saying is that there has been a real change, even though it's not so visible on the surface.'

Mary started to join in after she had removed the rest of the prawn crackers from my reach. 'It's like the Outer Hebrides and Welsh Revivals. They broke the religious system and infused life into the church, and even though you can hardly see the impact marks of either today, the dough mountain of church has been moved on by faith dynamic. Is that what you're getting at?'

We cleared up the dishes and I managed to burn myself on the little tea lights beneath the Chinese food warmers. Then we sat down with our coffee.

'Television or Scrabble?' questioned my son.

'No way!' I answered. 'Anything but Scrabble. Even talking.'

'Now there's a radical idea,' opinioned my sarcastic son, knowing my introverted nature.

As I hid behind Jeremy's *Daily Express*, I listened in to Mary's conversation with our son.

'Wallace was telling me that we were shortfalling by about £6,000 on our church budget this year. We were going to have a gift day, but do you know what happened?'

Jeremy emitted a vaguely encouraging noise.

'We had an email from Bishop Albert in Zambia, telling about that terrible famine and how it had hit their villages. It was totally heart-rending, thinking of our friend in the midst of such appalling things.'

'Yeah,' muttered our son in a passable imitation of his father.

'Well, we decided, instead of having a gift day to ask our church to help him – you know, send some money direct for food and seed and all that. After all, people dying is more important than worrying about our £6,000 budget shortfall. And do you know what happened? Well, the money we collected for Zambia amounted to well over that £6,000, and we sent it all off to Bishop Albert. We received some lovely pictures showing us how brilliant they thought our help was.' She concluded, 'We felt so good. It was such a blessing to us.'

Jeremy sat up. 'But what about the budget shortfall? What's happened to that?'

'That's the amazing thing,' said his mother. 'We got to the end of the year and the shortfall had totally disappeared. God just seemed to provide. Not only that, but strangely we found ourselves more than £6,000 in the black. Talk about pressed down and running over!'[1]

I put down the paper. 'That's exactly what I meant earlier. You know, when I was talking about my dough mountain. It was our faith dynamic – the faith dynamic of the church. Instead of just allowing the system to dictate our budget with sensible, normal credit and loss, we stood in faith; made an impression. Now, in a few months it will all have been forgotten and the imprint will have gone, but in the spiritual realm the mountain will have moved. Do you see?' I went on, 'We can't get hold of the system and just get rid of it. That's

---

[1] Luke 6:38.

not possible. But what we can do is move it and shake it with faith. And things will happen. All these small faith things that people are doing all over the place are slowly but surely reshaping the system, even though their work may seem, at the time, simply to fade into oblivion.'

Jeremy refilled my coffee cup and rescued his newspaper before I could fill in his crossword. He commented, 'It's like when we stood in faith against the Quinton Mob when we first came to Birmingham, and God sent those angels to sort it all out. Now it may seem as if it's all in the past and that's that, nothing to be seen. But that's not true, is it? The faith dynamic has moved us all on. It has impacted on people's lives, the spiritual realm and, through your book, churches all over the world. The mountain has been moved. Yes?'

Mary put my perception into biblical terms. 'You're right. The status quo, the system, the way things are, people's expectations of the church – they are just like a mountain and just as impossible to move.' She smiled. 'But look at what Jesus says: "If you have faith as small as a mustard seed, you can say to this mountain, 'Move from here to there' and it will move." '[2]

* * *

Man-created systems are important. We need a system to run a church, just as much as we need a system to run anything in this life, if we are to avoid anarchy. However, church systems that are embraced and then allowed to develop

[2] Matthew 17:20.

unchecked merely masquerade as light. They have a propensity to lead God's people away from the Light of the World. And, of course, they have a spiritual identity as well.

A wise ecclesiastical system ought to 'guard' the gospel[3] in a godly and positively helpful way. This will lead to the foundation of sound Christian ways. A good Christian inheritance links today's church with the authentic and inspirational men and women of the past 'commended for their faith',[4] so keeping us in touch with the 'glorious company of heaven'.[5] At the same time, the system should allow today's church to express worship so it communicates with contemporary society, and seeks to get across the essentials of our faith to the local community.

At its best, the system of church should celebrate and enliven that inherited golden thread of faith in Jesus Christ as Lord that streams through all time, yesterday, today and for ever, and yet make it accessible, spiritual and exciting for the rising generations.

It is not the system that is inherently bad. However, allowing the system to develop unchecked is wrong. The gospel faith dynamic must underpin and guide the system. If faith is the leader and the system is there to serve, then our Jesus can truly move mountains through his people.

---

[3] 1 Timothy 6:20.

[4] Hebrews 11:39.

[5] *Common Worship*, Eucharistic Prayer.

16
Gnats and Camels

Strain out a gnat but swallow a camel. (Matthew 23:24)

The devil loves to mess things up. He takes a perverted delight in twisting true teaching in the church. The forces of evil know fine well that a messed-up church will lead to a messed-up society and ultimately to unsaved generations. It was thus in the Old Testament, in the time of Jesus and in the long, complicated, sometimes heroic and often sad history of the church. To build a credible and germane church demands a stand against 'powers', and needs prophetic direction, as Jesus himself demonstrated . . .

The crowds gathered round Jesus as he spoke strongly yet softly: 'You must obey them [the scribes and Pharisees] and do everything they tell you.'

The crowd grew slightly restless and doubt appeared on their faces. 'Obey *them*?' they questioned each other. 'Is that what he wants us to do?'

'But do not do what they do, for they do not practise what they preach.'

A wave of humour swept through the crowd. Jesus had their full attention.

'He's got that right!' commented the local market trader.

'Wouldn't trust them with my mother-in-law, let alone my money.'

The crowd swayed forward to hear more.

'They tie up heavy loads and put them on men's shoulders, but they themselves are not willing to lift a finger to move them.'

The crowd looked appreciative. 'This man knows what he's talking about. Cut above you and me, they think themselves to be.'

Then Jesus' coup de grâce on the religious leaders: 'You blind guides! You strain out a gnat but swallow a camel.'[1]

The crowd broke down in hysterical laughter. Here was a man who spoke their language, yet also spoke the truth. Everyone knew that the religious system had become top heavy; that the Pharisees couldn't see beyond the end of their noses. They had become so preoccupied with the little gnats, the fine detail of their religious practice, that they'd missed whopping great camels that were steadily and strongly turning their temple practices into a nonsense.

'It's just like he said,' shouted a vineyard worker from Cana to anyone who would listen. 'Ever seen a poor Pharisee? But try to explain you just can't afford the outrageous prices they ask for their sacrifices and they won't listen. They're more interested in lining their pockets than the kingdom of God, if you ask me!'

The crowd shouted their appreciation with gusto.

'I can see what Jesus meant by those gnats,' stated Mary rocking gently back and forth on our friend's garden chair. As she spoke the swallows dived, narrowly missing the house eaves, and our friendly robin perched cheekily on the patio edge as the magpie proudly strutted round his domain. Two

---

[1] Matthew 23:3–4, 24.

or three rabbits sat statuesquely or dramatically ran from side to side about their mysterious business. An occasional jet thundered overhead on its escape from Manchester Airport. Mary and I sat in this idyllic English garden ruminating over gnats and camels.

'All those religious things that needed to be done to the nth degree – like not lifting a finger on the Sabbath.' She looked at me meaningfully as if to say, 'I know somebody who hardly lifts a finger in the house on any day of the week.'

'And I can see the "camel" Jesus talked about as well,' she continued. 'They simply didn't take any notice of what Jesus called the greatest commandments of the Old Testament. You know, like "Love the Lord your God with all your heart" and so on.' She looked at me. 'Do you see? The "greed and self-indulgence" of the Pharisees was a sign of them loving themselves more than God. And certainly more than others. He said they were "whitewashed tombs".'[2]

She frowned slightly. 'But what about now – the twenty-first century? What are today's gnats and camels?'

'It's obvious isn't it?' I countered without thought.

'Oh yeah? Come on then, my little oracle. Explain it all.'

I thought hard to retrieve the situation. 'Did you want your strawberries and cream now?'

Mary smiled indulgently. She knew the reason for my sudden change of conversation.

Looking round the church today, there are not so many 'gnats'. Few people are interested in the minutiae of religious practice. The Pharisee and his hypocritical ways has truly been put to bed. But there are 'camels' aplenty.

That evening, I sat flipping the TV remote in that semi-bored way. Working my way through a video of Harrison

---

[2] Matthew 23:25, 27.

Ford saving the world – again – fast-forwarding the boring parts, I came to the part where Ford's character has to enter the cave to retrieve the Holy Grail, which is a name for the chalice that Jesus supposedly used for the Last Supper. Of course, the 'baddy' greedily chooses the super-duper chalice, all gold and decorated with precious stones, and gets caught in a whirlwind of decay, dying in seconds. Our hero takes the coarse, wooden, carpenter's one and it proves to be correct. Surprise, surprise. But it does remind us plaintively of how today's church has sanitised the faith – made Christ decent, respectable, cosy and even snug. One example is our sanitised shepherds of the traditional nativity. Professor Jim Fleming remarks: 'The news was announced to homeless, dirty, smelly, landless shepherds . . . there were flies everywhere and sheep dung all over . . . get out of your head the romantic Christmas card . . .'[3]

In our largely middle-class Western church, we have made Christianity 'nice': comfortable seats and comfortable messages, helpful peer groups, excellent worship groups and pleasant friends; pretty crosses to wear round our necks or to hang at the front of sometimes beautiful church buildings. And, supremely, a tolerantly loving acceptance of all of society's ways.

Yet the Bible reminds us that the cross is an 'offence'[4] to natural thinking. Jesus died with nails hammered through his body and gouges from the whipping; with a crown of terrible thorns thrust down onto his skull and in the midst of a crowd baying for blood. One of the first Christians was pitilessly stoned to death and the others forced to flee for their

---

[3] Professor James Fleming, 'James Son of Joseph, Brother of Jesus, Ossuary'. (Biblical Archaeology Society).

[4] Galatians 5:11.

lives. Christians, we are told by historians, were covered in oil and 'spiked' on Emperor Nero's fence and lit to serve as human torches. Others were sewn up in animal skins and fed helplessly to the wild animals. They tell us of Christian families being fed to the lions in the arenas, often with the children being the first victims.

We have been hoodwinked into accepting decorous interpretations coming out of various historical worldviews, because they are so comfortable and so tolerant. The offence of the cross has been sanitised to fit in, and everything is oh so reasonable. Well, let me tell you, Christianity is not reasonable. Our 'camel' almost commands the church to fit in with society rather than tell of God's radical way forward for his people. And, as we fit in, so we lose the fear of the Lord. We lose the awesomeness of our God. We lose the amazingness of what it truly means to be a Christian. We lose the astonishment of what it means to be forgiven and saved. We lose the sense of the 'otherness' of God as he is reduced to the acceptable, ordinary and worldly.

I came and sat on the edge of Mary's bed later that evening and tried to share my thoughts with her. However, she had obviously been thinking along the same lines and was full of parallel ideas. 'Let's face it,' she said strongly, 'the church has dumbed down. We've lost the fear of the Lord, our values are all over the place, and we've embraced the individualistic needs-based culture rather than the absolutes of the gospel.' She looked quite ferocious for a moment. 'We are so afraid of being seen to judge anybody that our level of tolerance is almost unbelievable.' She ended with one of those irrefutable mini-statements: 'We are better at spin than truth.'

As Mary paused to take a sip of tea I tried to get a word in edgeways, but she was in full flow: 'Remember that

Methodist minister who was attacked outside his church and hospitalised? Then a year later, his attacker came to be god-parent to a mate's child, never dreaming he would meet the same minister. I can't think why. And Harvey just went ahead with it all, didn't he? He thought that his silent "loving" acceptance of the attacker would open up a pathway to God for the thug. He reduced the gospel of repentance and truth to a sanitised niceness. Never mind about the violence, the non-repentance, the drink on their breath or the hidden laughter over his gullibility. That was a camel if ever there was one – putting a spin on grace, and making God's love into some sort of sentimental slush.' Mary finished it all off in her usual teacher's voice: 'Jesus is shouting at us to sort out the camels that are destroying his church.'

* * *

Is your church swallowing a camel? Are you allowed to fill your minds with small matters, while losing sight of the fact that men, women and children are missing out on salvation? Is your church aware that in Africa Christians are being persecuted, sometimes to death, while we go about our comfortable, prosperous faith? That Christians are starving, while obesity reigns in our 'gimme-more' Western society? Do we allow the camel of messed-up teaching to march through church and nation so that the Saviour looks at us and weeps? Is God's church truly a prophetic body speaking God's heart to the nation or merely a group of in-people looking after their personal needs while folk out there are dying in their sins?

Pastors and ministers, are you prophetic leaders or simply 'fillers of need', in self and others? Are you driven more by personal and church success than the fear of the Lord? Are you shortsightedly focused on the gnat of personal position and self-pride? Have you yourself become a blind guide?

Over the centuries, God has raised up prophetic leaders to drive his church away from following the worldly spirit of the age and becoming enslaved by ecclesiastical systems; to stand up and slaughter the 'camels' in his church. Take the examples of two Johns – separated by more than 200 years . . .

* * *

The children were very noisy. Wherever you went in Susannah's small house, it was filled with hubbub and the vibrancy of life. She had little time for herself in an era without cleaning devices or automatic washing machines. Her life was choked with the heavy drudge of housework. This was more than an excuse to miss out on prayer and allow her faith to cool, but Susannah Wesley was a praying woman. In the midst of that crowded kitchen she spent time with the Lord by pulling her apron over her head and creating personal space.

Her son, John, went to Oxford and helped form the incredible 'holy club'. He was ordained as a priest of the Church of England and then went off in 1735 to Georgia as a missionary. It was when he returned home after a fraught and seemingly powerless ministry that he happened upon a small church in Aldersgate Street in London.

Imagine, for a moment, John sitting there on the hard,

straight-backed pew, feeling 'What's the point? Where is this God anyway?' – disillusioned by years of seemingly pointless work and grinding discipline. Perhaps he was shouting at God within his spirit.

Then there was one of those rare, transcendent moments, like Isaiah when he said, 'I saw the Lord seated on a throne'[5] or Ezekiel when he commented, 'The Spirit came into me and raised me to my feet',[6] and John was overwhelmed by the power and presence of God. He would later write in classic understatement: 'I felt I did trust in Christ, Christ alone for salvation . . .'[7] Perhaps he immediately dashed back to the family house, shouting at Susannah, 'Mother, I've met him! It's true! Jesus really is alive!'

John Wesley, with his gifting of an apostolic ministry, wrestled with the boundaries of the Anglican church for many years. But the system was just too strong in its establishment power, so he was almost forced to set up the Methodist congregations. It was not that John Wesley had an anarchistic streak or that he did not value the authority of the church. It was simply that the system had become so inward-looking that it had to be broken to enable the revivalist Spirit of God to be released on the people.

In complete contrast to John Wesley, a twentieth-century John was being 'raised a pagan – a fourth generation unbeliever – having never entered a church before the age of 29'.[8] When he met with Christ, he was a successful jazz musician. The story goes of how John Wimber, the subsequent founder of the Vineyard church movement, sought to become part of

---

[5] Isaiah 6:1.

[6] Ezekiel 2:2.

[7] Raymond Brown, *Four Spiritual Giants* (Kingsway).

[8] John Wimber, *Power Evangelism* (Hodder & Stoughton).

the established church and yet met with a religious system that totally trivialised and marginalised anything to do with the supernatural. 'How can this be,' he questioned, 'when God himself is supernatural? Ridiculous!'

Yet through his obedient ministry and the breaking down of man-made boundaries, the whole church has been profoundly blessed by the restoration of deep-felt worship, together with the pouring out of gifts of the Holy Spirit. Of course, that movement, like all other establishments, stands continually in danger of becoming a system that will itself need to be reformed.

Of course, we are not called to be Wesleys or Wimbers, but as the people of God we are continually called to look afresh at the religious 'stuff' and ensure that it points towards the living Lord. Slavery to a system pulls us down into the abyss of legalistic rules and regulations, which can lead to that acute tiredness of spirit that comes from serving the world under the guise of obedience to the Lord of glory. Rather, we are continually called to make the gospel accessible to all.

Twenty-first-century Christianity is no different in fundamentals to the first-century model. Just as they struggled with the world, the flesh and the devil, so must we. Society, in its fallen nature, will always tend towards deviation rather than truth, holiness and loveliness. Put one bad apple in a barrel of a hundred and the worm will have its way.

The church of God is a wonderful institution, and I delight to be an Anglican Christian. But I am under no illusion: my denomination is flawed and partly broken. I work within a church that is, in David Watson's words, a 'hospital for sinners'. I offer a right and proper allegiance to that organisation, but I owe my heart to my Lord and Saviour, Jesus Christ.

17
The Sausage Machine

Now you are the body of Christ, and each one of you is a part of it. (1 Corinthians 12:27)

It hurts when cherished false comforts are attacked.

I like to think that I am tidy and careful in my ways. Mary tells me otherwise.

I prefer to imagine that my preaching is of consistently high standard – until I catch a sneaking glimpse of somebody nodding off.

I want to believe that I am an excellent counsellor – until somebody gets angry with me for not listening properly.

I considered that evangelicals were the best of the Anglican bunch – until the Lord spoke to me about my prejudices . . .

* * *

'There's no way I'm going to any convention like that,' I forcefully stated to Martin and Janet Knox. 'I'm far too busy here in the parish. Who's going to do my work? I mean, look at my diary. We even missed our day off last week.' I looked at Mary because I knew this last point would help my case.

But she was not forthcoming. In fact she totally ignored my argument and was looking at me in a sort of pitying way. 'No, Wallace. You've simply got it all wrong,' she enunciated. 'You're really pleased that the bishop wanted your input into that Urban Priority Area conference, but you have trouble with other people's ways of ministry. If you don't go to the conference, it won't be because you're too busy. It'll be because of your attitude to the non-evangelicals. You know that's right, don't you?' she added forcefully.

The convention was held at a massive Victorian red-brick, gothic-style, gaunt-yet-strangely-moving country mansion. I carried my bags into the dark, oak-encrusted hall with the smell of history. On the wall hung the inevitable badly painted portrait of some distant benefactor looking down with a benevolent grimace.

Other delegates were arriving. Most seemed to be dressed in black. And worse still, from my point of view, they seemed to know each other. Their ringing laughter left me feeling like a bleak outsider. After registering, I slipped off to my cheerless, lonely 'cell'.

Chapel was next on the agenda. As I arrived, I realised I had forgotten to bring my prayer book, so I walked in apprehensively and sat down. Everybody else, as far as I could see, not only had their prayer book open at the right page, but had also genuflected, crossed themselves several times and spent an inordinate length of time kneeling in silent prayer. This prayerful reflection was followed by further crossing of themselves until they sat with perfect composure and serene expression, waiting for worship to commence. On the other hand, I had sudden cognisance of my own slouched position, that I hadn't bothered to pray, had pins and needles in my left leg and had a mind full of criticism.

As the evening wore on, I convinced myself that their

expression was merely outward, while mine, albeit unwholesome, was authentic and realistic. I consoled myself with the understanding that the few evangelicals present were the ones who were biblical, sound and right. But here were the horns of my dilemma. I believed God was calling me to a wider leadership, but how could I minister with love and truth to ministers of different traditions and denominations when really, in my heart of hearts, I clung to the idea of mine being the better way?

As the convention continued, my confidence began to slip. I found myself profoundly impressed by the spirituality of my 'catholic' brethren and even by the intellectual prowess of the liberal church people. Furthermore, I was disappointed that the input by the small number of evangelicals was often shallowly simplistic.

'Well?' questioned Mary as I arrived home.

'I don't know. I'm confused,' I answered. 'Everything was so straightforward until I went. I don't know if I can ignore the way other leaders approach God any more. It's made me think.'

'Excellent,' replied my wife in a flagrantly provoking tone – as if she knew this would happen all along. 'About time too.' I grunted morosely, trudged upstairs and had a long, hot, self-pitying bath.

* * *

The questions deepened for me as we motored through France, and then on to Geneva and into Italy. On the one hand it was so brilliant to shed my professional role and simply enjoy sunshine and leisure. Yet as we climbed the ancient, weather-beaten steps into the magnificent Tuscan church buildings, the uncertainties returned. In the otherwise glorious churches, Jesus always appeared as the dead man on the cross and the eternal baby of the virgin, rather than our present-day, resurrected, ascended Saviour and Lord. What a contrast between the beautiful countryside of Tuscany, with its wonderfully stylish church buildings, and the sense of darkness and death I perceived within them. How could I accept this way of being church as credible and important?

'Let's stop off at Taizé on the way home,' said Mary. 'See what that sort of place says to us.'

Taizé is an interdenominational monastery famed for its sung worship, having a modern style yet full of the richness of the past, and certainly not in the classic evangelical mould. As we entered the contemporary building and sat cross-legged on the hard floor, my spirit immediately soared. The hundreds of candles complemented the wafting colourful drapes, and the carefully choreographed procession of the elegantly robed monks was stunning as they chanted their biblically based worship.

God spoke to me profoundly, yet softly and gently, in my heart as I soared into some sort of seventh heaven. I 'saw' a slatted Venetian blind enshrouding a very bright window. For some reason the slats were totally closed, omitting all light. Then the Lord showed me the slats opened to various degrees. The light shone through to whatever degree the blind was opened. It was important that light was shining through, yet there was still darkness to whatever degree. I sensed God saying, 'It is important that light is in the church. Push aside the degree of darkness and understand where there is light. Even if it's surrounded by darkness, rejoice in the light.'

Later I staggered out of the building, my heart and head ringing with God's revelation. I realised with utter and miraculous comprehension that God had been speaking to me of his church. By focusing on the darkness, I had fixated my mind on my 'rightness' and failed to comprehend God in his radiant fullness and omnipotence. I had boxed God into the tinyness of my limited mind; blind to the broader picture. I was not rejoicing in the light that was there, but cynically dwelling on the negative. In consequence I had reduced God to my human proportions. How absolutely ridiculous to treat the King of creation in such a cavalier and hidebound fashion! I could do little but throw myself to my knees and pray repentantly, 'Lord, forgive my bigotedness – my unwholesome and limited view of your Person, and especially my small-minded perspective of your church. Please forgive me!'

* * *

We sat in the Knox household some days after our return, sharing a bottle of Chianti accompanied by large portions of French cheese. I was full of words about my startling religious experience at Taizé.

'I realise what's been happening,' I continued with gusto. 'It's not just about me – it applies to the whole church system. Do you remember, Mary, that when I felt called into the ministry, God led us to that particular college, and its ways became *the* way we did things – the right way?'

Mary agreed, 'Yes, you're right! It's as if the college ways became stamped somewhere in our souls – maybe subconsciously. I remember laughing with you and the others at the expense of the "high church" and scorning the lack of faith of the "liberals". We were the guys!'

Martin nodded. 'Of course, it was the same in my church as a lad. We used to pay lip service to all the others, but really we were where it was at.'

I continued thoughtfully, 'It was a bit like a sausage machine. In went the young trainees and out came your systemised minister. And then off to an evangelical parish that built upon those values, often without any real understanding or consideration of other expressions of faith.'

'But hold on a moment,' chortled Janet with an ironic smile. 'Doesn't that mean all minsters are a product of their background and their college and their training?'

'Nurture or nature?' muttered Martin. He continued, 'I think each of us, almost naturally, sees our strand as more authentic.'

'Yes, that's right,' I agreed. 'But what God's saying to me is that I must learn to value his truth in all those other strands, and not make ridiculous judgements, often from ignorance of their ways. He told me, Martin, simply to glory in the light of Christ.' I ended, 'It's so amazingly releasing!'

Mary added adroitly, 'It's as if we were in slavery to a system.'

* * *

This is not some plea for soft-bellied ecumenism. In the past, that movement has tended to bundle all expressions of faith together into one frail and weak common denominator. And because of that fatal flaw, it has been sidelined by many. God's vision to me at Taizé luxuriates in the wonderful variety and diversity wrought by him. As the people of God, we are to rejoice in the light that has been given to us personally, yet also learn to rejoice in the light elsewhere. That's not to say we don't have to recognise and fight the darkness – St Paul makes that so very clear.[1] It's more of an attitude to the totality of God. He is everything and all in all.

Mary is a great C. S. Lewis fan and reminds me of his incisive story in *The Great Divorce* of a famous artist in 'heaven'. The 'spirit' tells the artist how every Christian has something amazingly individualistic to teach about an aspect of God's character and that we need to be really grateful to those who are and do things differently from us; to realise that they are showing us something wonderful about God that they have got hold of and we haven't. And vice versa. 'There'll be some things which you'll see better than anyone else. One of the things you'll want to do will be to tell us about them,' says that same 'spirit' of Lewis's narrative. He so brilliantly illustrates God's plan of every Christian contributing towards a joined-up understanding of the totality of God. So it is with the streams of faith as they look towards him.

So, I have to acknowledge: I've been sausage machined! Not intentionally, but because we all need a system and model in which to work out our ministry. But I woke up one morning after my Taizé experience and found that all my individualistic ways were far from the full picture, and that I must seek and rejoice in the fullness of God revealed within all the streams and churchmanships of the Christian faith, as well as remaining certain of my personal calling to my own understanding.

So what are the implications? I am caught up in a system. I fancy that I am basking in the freedom of the Spirit, but in

---

[1] Ephesians 6:10f.

reality my thoughts and ways and model of ministry are incomplete and flawed, as indeed, in my humanity, they must be. I need to relearn my relationship with other Christians and delight in their spirituality, even though it may be different from mine. That is the way of dynamic faith.

Further, the church itself is also caught up, because you and I and others are the church. And we are surely a separate and disparate lot! Indeed, if we are all systemised by our various strands, does that mean the church in totality is hidebound to a gigantic system that holds its people in slavery rather than liberating them to luxuriate in the Persons of the Godhead?

And is there a connection here with Mary's cobweb picture? Is part of the enemy's cobweb spun on the independence and pride of the various strands of faith expression? Does God weep in heaven because his children refuse to love their siblings? At the end times, will God stop to ask the people rising into glory, 'Well, which denomination were you?' before he opens the pearly gate?

I am indebted to Nick Cuthbert, the founder of Riverside Church in Birmingham, for his far-sighted comment on true church unity called 'One Church – Many Congregations'.

But it's not merely a matter of talk and action plans. It has to come from an inner conviction that God's light is shown, to some extent, through all the streams, and that together we make up the one river of God's holy people. We shall beat the system and tear away the cobwebs through knowledge and love followed by proactive decision.

But do not imagine for one moment that the devil will stand on the sidelines . . .

18
Looking for the Light

> And I pray that you, being rooted and established in love, may have power, together with all the saints, to grasp how wide and long and high and deep is the love of Christ, and to know this love that surpasses knowledge – that you may be filled to the measure of all the fulness of God. (Ephesians 3:17–19)

The faded noticeboard made up my mind: 'PARISH EUCHARIST – 9.30 AM'. I didn't want to go.

Mary looked pleased when I made the statement, even though the church looked quintessentially English, and one could almost hear the Sunday peal of bells.

'I haven't brought my hat anyway,' she quipped. The picture in her mind, as clear as in mine, was of tight permed hair-dos, smothered by the obligatory hat and laced with tailored 'Sunday best'. The whole effect of the Sunday ladies shaking the limp hand of the ineffectual vicar was too strong. Equally shocking, the parody might even be true! It was the simple words 'Parish Eucharist' that fed our minds with anticipation of boredom rather than glory.

'But I really would like to go to church,' she continued after our unspoken thoughts took root. 'It's still Sunday tomorrow, holiday or not.'

'Well, how about their sung evensong at 6.30 pm?' I offered with impish humour as we drove back to our holiday cottage.

The following day, we ended up at the local primary school. A partly obscured flyer in the high street offered us the chance to 'worship Jesus'. Our natural curiosity about church life and a sense that here was an opportunity to meet some purposeful Christians motivated us – unlike the 'Parish Eucharist' advert. Yet I do see the Eucharist (holy communion) as central to the Christian expression of worship, so questions surely need to be asked about our presentation of ourselves.

'Praise the Lord! Come on in!' beamed the welcomer. 'Where do you come from? How's your holiday going? Praise the Lord!'

We sat tentatively on the junior school chairs as the worship band noisily got the sound system right after producing a full quota of banshee wails. Then smiling beamer number two welcomed us again, 'especially our visitors' as he looked significantly at Mary and me. All eyes followed.

'Thank goodness I didn't tell them I'm a vicar!' I whispered to Mary when I should have been jumping up and down and praising the Lord.

Communion time came along and absolute chaos ensued: everyone feeding everybody else; hugs, kisses, half-hour chats. Smiling beamer number three 'blessed' us and at least half a dozen people offered us mangled bits of bread or a sip of Ribena.

Yet it was also brilliant. Here was a group of people who, as far as one could tell, were devoted to the Lord as well as each other. There was a spontaneity and joy emanating from their togetherness that was the very antitheses of the feeling within us summed up by 'Parish Eucharist'.

Mary put it succinctly: 'I'm not sure I could cope with it every Sunday, but it somehow expressed the New Testament church to me. It had the vitality and life that's so often missing from our stereotyped Anglican stuff.'

We sat in a lovely chintzy café later, feeling slightly guilty about abusing Sunday trading, and enjoyed an equally illegal cholesterol feast.

'So has our churchy system killed that vitality of worship?' I asked Mary through the high fat crumbs.

'Well, I certainly didn't miss the pews and the maudlin hymns,' she replied. 'But don't forget, Wallace, what the Lord taught us through Taizé. You have to be so careful not to be narrow-minded and judgemental.'

And she was right. It would be easy and certainly superficial to use such an anecdote to damn the modern established church. And it was only a short time later that we shared in a completely different type of worship.

We entered the Holy Rood church. It looked quite wonderful. The sheer colour and symbolism of the classically curved ceiling was set off by the clouds of incense that swirled numinously around the nave. The feeling was one of awe and reverence for a holy God. Not a place for foolish laughter or glib comments, but of sitting back and being consumed by the transcendent nature of the heavenly Father. The walls and furnishings shouted into the soul, and even the priest's demeanour as he crawled on his belly towards the altar spoke profoundly of a God who is beyond and unapproachable in his absoluteness. Here was an experience of God in the exact opposite corner to the new church in the primary school. The Holy Rood Eucharist was powerful and uplifting.

Could both be right at the same time? Mary sorted my mind out. 'It's like you found through Taizé. God is not merely in one or the other,' she explained to me as we boarded the train for our journey back to Birmingham. 'He's both and everything else, all at the same time. Those services were showing us something equally valid and equally exciting about the nature of God. Do you see?'

We found our pre-booked seat numbers.

Mary continued, 'It's that "both at the same time" that really gets non-Christian people. That's why they talk about the so-called contradictions of Christianity. You often hear people say things like, "How can God be merciful and yet consign people to hell at the same time?" or "How can God be good if the world is evil" – don't you?'

'Yes,' I admitted like a schoolboy.

'It's because God is a paradox,' she continued with earnest expression. 'He is everything – all at the same time. He developed the early church with amazing signs and wonders and yet allowed Stephen to be cruelly stoned to death. He used the Ark of the Covenant as a power box, and then killed that Israelite – what was his name again? – when he dared to touch the side of it.'[1] She looked at me almost tearfully. 'Don't you see? It's one of the reasons why I love the Lord. God is always greater than any human situation.'

It was quite snug, really, sitting in the first-class carriage, chatting about God – even getting called for a meal together in the dining car. Oh the joys of off-peak travel and having a son who earns enough to give us treats.

As the non-packet soup arrived, Mary continued: 'It's just like that writer said – the one you like – you cannot put God into a box.'

'Oh, you mean William Barclay. Yes. He says we always want to bring God down to our level of thinking; put a

---

[1] 2 Samuel 6:7.

system round him, to contain him and keep him "tame". But it's like C. S. Lewis says as well, he's not tame but he is safe'.[2] I continued with hardly a breath, 'Isn't that just the trouble with the church in general? It wants to systemise Almighty God – put him into its plans and methods and sort him out – whereas the reality is that he is beyond all such paltriness.'

I thought a bit as the waiter offered the pudding. 'So what is true worship then?'

Mary merely sighed.

* * *

I always like to bring what God has been showing me back into the everyday life of the church, and this is one of the reasons why I find the set readings of the Anglican lectionary so hard to live with. Of course there is a reverse, paradoxical side, as Mary would be quick to point out with reference to her C. S. Lewis 'bible'. He brilliantly tells us about the minister who week in week out pursues his own preferences and ends up on a smaller and smaller repeating cycle of his favourite hymns and Bible readings.[3]

So, pushing aside the organised theme the following Sunday morning, I spoke out about my new understandings. 'God gave me this vision of a shuttered window,' I shared with them, 'and then said, "Rejoice in the amount of light you perceive shining through, whether it be great or small." I think he means us to look for faith in the part of his church where they do things differently from us.'

---

[2] C. S. Lewis, *The Lion, the Witch and the Wardrobe.*

[3] C. S. Lewis, *Screwtape Letters.*

I'd managed to borrow an incense swinger from a high church colleague in a neighbouring parish, which I had inexpertly lit in the vestry beforehand. I brought it out with a dramatic flourish. 'Do you know what the Bible tells us about incense?' I asked rhetorically. '"The smoke of the incense, together with the prayers of the saints, went up before God from the angel's hand."[4] We are Bible-believing Christians, so why don't we use incense?'

Unfortunately a partial answer to my question was already becoming apparent. The smoke was gushing forth in a great cloud. My lighting had obviously been over-successful, due to my total lack of expertise. And people started to splutter and cough dramatically – over-dramatically to my mind.

But the point was made. The church became committed to 'seeing light', happily acknowledging 'how wide and long and high and deep is the love of Christ', together with a new appreciation of the 'otherness' of God, while retaining their evangelical identity.

* * *

'Seeing light' in other Christians and other Christian streams is also painful and paradoxical, as well as a beautiful expression of Jesus' exhortation to love one another . . .

The Christian young man clearly wanted to talk about a deep issue. I could see the intensity lining his expression. 'Could I just have a few minutes to chat about something?' he asked with undivided concern.

---

4 Revelation 8:4.

'No problem, Neil,' I replied. 'How about we meet in the coffee shop in Harborne tomorrow morning? Can you make that?' I had a sense that the issue this dynamic Christian man wanted to discuss was better brought out on neutral ground. A vicar's study can be very intimidating.

I stirred my cappuccino thoroughly as Neil falteringly started to speak. 'Wallace, I've got to tell you that I'm gay.' He looked at me as if the sky were about to fall down as a consequence of his revelation. I could understand why he was worried. It seems to me that we evangelical Christians are often hard, cold and forbidding about this issue. Cut and dried and sorted.

'Tell me about it,' I said, feeling inwardly panicky. I fumbled slightly with the toasted tea cake. What should I say? What did I really believe and would my belief bear inspection?

'You know I'm a Christian?' Neil questioned as he, in turn, fiddled with his doughnut.

I realised he was looking wan, and what a question! Of course I knew he was a Christian. He was a brilliant, lovely, exciting, dynamic Christian. But it had become a question. What was happening inside this young man of faith? Did he expect me to reject him, and tell him his faith was invalid?

'But I have these feelings, you see. They're just inside me no matter how hard I try to reject them. The truth is, I only get turned on by other men. It's how I am. I like women, but they are just . . . women.' The words poured out across the little circular coffee table. 'I've always been like that. Always. It's just me. I'm not a pervert. I'm just me. And I do love the Lord. Don't you see?'

Into my confused mind flashed the words God had given me: 'Look for the light – rejoice in the light.'

'Neil,' I said, reaching out for his hand with no regard to

the other coffee drinkers. 'Neil, I know you love the Lord. I know you are a Christian. The light is there for all to see. And Neil, I love you as well. Just as Jesus loves you – just as you are!'

There are many issues surrounding homosexuality. Not least in the evangelical churches' rejection of gay people. Over the centuries we have categorised, stereotyped and almost demonised men and women for no reason other than they have been born with a sexual orientation that is not conventional. If we are talking about repentance, then it is first and foremost the church system that needs to put its house in order and turn away from judgemental imperatives. Being gay is not a sin.

At the same time, I believe that sodomy is wrong. It appears to be the reason why God brought his judgement on Sodom.[5] But then it is no more wrong than the whole list of things that 'make a man unclean' such as 'sexual immorality, theft . . . greed, malice, deceit . . . envy, slander' and so on.[6] And the very idea of senior church leaders being in any such obvious, active sin, without any sense of repentance, I find to be outrageous.

The paradox is that we are called to love people where they are, not where we think they ought to be. Perhaps it is this very paradox that makes me rejoice to be a member of the wider church in England. As I have written to my bishop:

> As a priest, I think it most important that I keep my views with personal integrity. At the same time I am totally committed to the unity of the church and see myself as part of the broad stream that shows the breadth and width of Christ's body on

---

[5] Genesis 19.

[6] Mark 7:21–23.

> earth. I therefore rejoice to join with Christians of other 'persuasions'. Of course, there is a tension in this position, but maybe it is also a godly tension as the church explores its own sin of the past in its equally wrong attitude to gay people . . . At the same time, I have to say what I have to say.[7]

Neil was oblivious to such erudite theological discussion. All he knew as we talked over the coffee table was that he loved Jesus, yet had clear feelings towards other men. 'Repent!' I hear my fellow Christians shout. Yet what has he to repent of other than original sin – in company with every man, woman and child (except our Saviour) who was ever born?

'Neil,' I said, 'I think homosexual love-making is wrong, but no more wrong than any other sin. I don't know what to answer you. I just feel I am committing you to a life of celibacy, and maybe that is the answer, but it seems very impossible. What do you think?'

'I think that nobody is helping me, that's what I think,' Neil replied without the slightest suggestion of bitterness. He was just stating a fact. And I think he was right. My answer was not an answer but a position.

'Neil, be sure of this,' I replied inadequately. 'God has told me to see the light in you. The Scriptures assure me of his love for you, and I think you are a brilliant Christian man. But I don't really know the way forward. Can you help me to understand?'

God is a speaking God. He speaks in many ways: through Scripture, holy communion, dreams, pictures, other people and even our frail human senses. And we powerfully need to learn to see the Christ light in others as we develop a greater sense of God's wonderful grace to all people; and we need to

---

[7] Email to Bishop of Worcester, 1st July 2003.

listen to God and each other. The light that is Christ always shines in the darkness[8] and the mountain of the system is brought down to size. As we listen to Jesus and to one another, the devil is forbidden a doorway and love prevails.

However, a new stage was opening up for Mary and me – an opportunity to widen our ministry. It was time go on 'The Tour' . . .

---

[8] John 1:5.

19
The Tour

> I pray that you may be active in sharing your faith, so that you will have a full understanding of every good thing we have in Christ. (Philemon 6)

The old lady with the greasy black coat strode determinedly along the litter-strewn asphalt pathway shadowed by the massive tower blocks. Her hair was slightly balding and straggly, and she wobbled somewhat because of her obese frame. There were plenty of chips inside her, I thought carelessly. I particularly noticed her dog. It was a huge Alsatian, and in its slobbering jaws lay a battered leather purse, while its mistress toted a soiled carrier bag.

Mary and I were on 'The Tour': A roadshow making its way around more than a score of major towns and cities talking about taking the gospel to 'the hidden poor', the disempowered people of the so-called British underclass who live on our 'sink' council estates. We had arrived quite early and the meeting rooms were still being readied for the incoming ministers, leaders and pastors, so we went for a walk around the 'difficult' area to get the hang of the place.

'I cannot believe anybody lives in that house,' said Mary. The front had been liberally 'egged', a ragged three-piece suite adorned the pathway and bits of broken wood lay everywhere, evidencing the previous night's skateboard 'jumping' track. And the surrounding neighbourhood, as we looked towards the concrete tower blocks, was little better. It was a living example of the need for Jesus to come in his power to the poor and needy.

The lady pounded her way towards us, and because I had my dog collar on, I said, 'Good morning. How are you?'

She stopped and looked at me. 'Are you the Father, Father?' she questioned.

I sort of nodded vaguely. It was too complicated.

'It's those bloody kids, you know. Drive me to an early grave they will! Can't you do something about it, Father?'

'Yes?' I volunteered.

'Bloody well banging on my window again last night. Not bloody right, is it?'

'No.'

'Nobody bloody cares anyway.' She sniffed loudly. 'That's what I thinks anyway.'

'Do you know your dog has your purse in its mouth?' I asked lamely.

'Course I bloody well do. Bloody kids, they're like animals around here. Pinch yer purse as soon as look at ya. But not from him they won't!' She looked lovingly down at him and caringly stroked his huge muzzle.

For my new friend, the kids were the animals and the animal was the friend. She trusted her Alsatian and despised the local children. In the darkness of 'living' she saw no light and safety except through her canine companion.

* * *

The seminars went really well, especially as we were able to introduce this bit of local 'colour'. And then we went back with the vicar to her estate vicarage round the corner.

'I've been here three years now,' she remarked plaintively, 'and I still feel like a fish out of water. I don't fit in on the estate. I'm not like them. Not better, you understand, just different. And my colleagues and even my family just don't understand what it's like.' Jenny looked wistful. 'I sometimes feel they can't cope with my needs. They have so many of their own. And I know some of them feel a sort of guilt because I'm living here and they have comfortable homes. It doesn't make sense, but there you are. I have no friends I can relate to in the church and all the other vicars seem either too busy or too exhausted. I just feel completely isolated and abandoned.'

Jenny paused to scratch a mark off her woolie. Then she lifted her eyes and I saw the tears.

The devil is alive and active in our so-called civilised society of today. We have just emerged from the most bloodthirsty (so I'm told) century that has ever been, yet the twenty-first century seems to offer no greater hope. And that hopelessness seems to manifest itself in many of our huge estates. It's as if humanity has lost its soul and become animalistic, even though, as the old lady pointed out, her animal was 'a better person'. Surely the devil looks on and smiles.

Jenny suffers from a not uncommon problem. She is isolated: a middle-class person, by training and lifestyle, set in a different culture. Also, at college, Jenny had been told, 'Don't make friends in the parish, because it will just create jealousies.' And anyway, her particular people are of a quite different peer group.

Further, she is clergy. She is a paid Christian leader – separate; different; in charge; 'holy', in some peoples eyes. Even in a middle-class environment, people nudge each other and stop swearing or bitching or whatever and become plastic replicas of respectability. Somehow, the church has succeeded in producing a separate 'leader' class, despite its call for all believers to be a 'royal priesthood'.[1]

Jenny smiled gratefully at us for listening. It wasn't much really. Just a friendly face and a willing ear.

I said naughtily, 'Jenny, whatever you do don't tell your bishop. You will go into the little mental box marked "able vicar but slightly neurotic".'

Mary emitted an enraged roar. 'What an absolutely outrageous statement!'

'Yes,' I smiled at Jenny, 'but keep your counsel.'

When we awoke the next morning, Jenny had carefully laid out breakfast and disappeared to sort out the world. The tea, I noticed, was herbal – something like 'Rosemary and Vile' – and the breakfast was muesli with skimmed milk. 'Delicious,' I muttered while searching cupboards for butter and anything unhealthy. At length I found some proper tea and even sugar. The day wasn't going to be so bad.

'Jenny,' I commented as we sat down with our decaffeinated coffee and 'hi-fibre' bars, 'the devil is always wanting to isolate us Christians; separate us from the body so he can pick us off.'

Mary nodded, 'Even the disciples were sent out two by two.'

'I was talking to some enthusiastic Christians the other week at a conference, and they were telling me how they meet for breakfast and prayer every week – just a few of them together. "It's made such an incredible difference in our lives and especially our personal spirituality," they said to me,

---

[1] 1 Peter 2:9.

more than once.' I looked at Jenny. 'Would that sort of thing work for you? Do you know anybody whom you could meet with? – perhaps commit to meeting with on a regular basis?'

Jenny looked thoughtful. 'Well, yes, I suppose so. But where can I find the time? And would it be honest to my people? And I'd have to go quite some distance.'

Mary put in, 'Practical Christianity means practical action. You have to do it – not just sit and wait for the answer to come to you. You are feeling isolated and vulnerable, so pray and act. That's how it should be.'

'What about you guys?' countered Jenny. 'But I suppose you have each other.'

'Well yes, we do. But sometimes we just accentuate our own needs rather than draw out an answer.'

Mary put in, 'You see, I know how Wallace will react and he knows how I will want to deal with things. There are different sorts of loneliness and isolation, even in a good marriage.'

'So how do you deal with it all?' asked our earnest hostess.

* * *

'How *do* we deal with it, Mary?' I asked my wife later on that evening as we journeyed further north.

'It goes back to the Lord, doesn't it? Remember how we prayed for about two years simply for somebody to come and help us? I mean we knew nobody in Birmingham apart from a few of my relatives. And then he sent us Martin and Janet Knox, remember? Amazing, wasn't it, when they just rang up out of the blue that time when we had returned from holiday and felt quite downcast? "Can we come and see you?" they said. "We think the Lord might be calling us to work with you in Birmingham." We hadn't even heard of them, let alone known them.'[2]

We stopped in the Lake District at a wonderful country pub. Chips and caffeine and salt were high on my agenda.

'But we had to step out to them, didn't we? Meet them halfway and form a relationship. God and us working together. That's what I like.'

'Like that man said, "Pray to God and keep your powder dry,"' I responded. 'God helps those who help themselves.'

'So where does it say that in the Bible?' smiled my always accurate wife.

I just smeared the steak with mustard.

It concerns me greatly that the system of the church is so isolationary. Ministers are trained, often by default, to be one-person leaders. Separated from 'real' life as professional Christians, they often spend long hours in isolated studies, and many have no daytime colleagues, but soldier on under often impossible circumstances. I notice that when curates start their ministry with me their assumptions are always towards separation, and I have great difficulty selling the concept of working out of a parish office or even sharing a ministry. Collaboration and accountability are often foreign to men and women who have generally made their way, very successfully, in industry, commerce or education. Not because they do not see joined-up working as the correct way, but because of status quo assumptions. That's the way they have seen their minister doing his work, as well as, far too often, representing the sub-surface training college model of ministry. God has also set us in families. We are to be collaborative, synergetic and together in mission and ministry.

---

[2] See *Angels on the Walls*.

As 'The Tour' continued, we stopped at a Glasgow estate. The ministers were bemoaning their lot. I remember an elderly man saying in strong Glaswegian: 'Och, man, dinnae take so much on yoursels. We're all in this together. It's about time you folks learnt that the Lord calls all of us to the ministry.'

Isolationism and separation of leaders has become the curse of the modern church. The system disconnects people and can lead to the totally ungodly division of deacons or clergy and 'punters' that besets our church practices today. It's good to have ministers and pastors, or whatever else we choose to call our leaders of today, but we are not a breed apart. We are part of the wonderful royal priesthood working in union to grow the kingdom of God for all people. We are family – we are one.

God calls all Christians to a collaborative ministry. Of course, Mary and I had seen teamwork as something 'idealistic' to pontificate on and to practise, to a degree, with Martin and Janet Knox. But God was about to upset the comfortable status quo of our nuclear family . . .

* * *

Mary and I had taken to praying with a clergy friend of ours, Christine Waudby. It was brilliantly refreshing to meet in her Black Country house, away from our parish, and pray together. I remember one night in particular as we sat quietly together waiting on God . . .

'It's Psalm 68:6,' pronounced Mary out of the blue, in her 'this is how it is, whatever you might think' tone of voice. She smiled knowingly from the recesses of Christine's comfortable pink damask settee. I was startled because I'd sunk into my normal exhausted mode and was thinking about what would be on TV. Christine raised her eyebrows. She knew Mary of old, and how God will often speak to her by putting a specific Bible reference in her mind, when she has no idea of the actual verse content. It generally works!

Christine picked up her Bible. 'I don't believe this,' she immediately commented. 'It's just what God has been saying to me. I don't believe it,' she repeated.

'Come on then, what does it say?' I questioned, now fully awake.

'"God sets the lonely in families", is what it says.'

We all knew immediately what it meant, even though we were shy about voicing it because it seemed so extreme by the standards of today's society. Christine was the sole survivor of her family bloodline. Her father had died recently and she had absolutely no close living relatives – no family. And here was God plainly saying to us that we had to become her family. It was an outrageous thought, yet it resounded in all souls. I voiced it first: 'Christine, you have to move into our vicarage as part of the family. We'll have to live as a sort of community.'

'Not only that,' Mary joined in. 'I think we have to have a joint ministry as well. Give up your present job and come and work alongside us. You can afford it with all the money that's been left to you.'

Now Christine is not one to be told what to do. She is a strong-minded woman with her own ideas. And furthermore, she had never lived with anyone since leaving home to go to teacher training college and then to teach in Leicester – where we had met her and brought her back to the Lord. So I expected fireworks.

'It's right,' she almost immediately commented, which is

amazing for Christine because she likes to ponder and then ponder again, and maybe again one more time.

'How do we test this out?' I asked, anxious not to make an incredible blunder that could ruin Christine's life.

Mary replied, 'That's easy. We'll ask our children. If Christine is to be part of our family, then they need to be her family as well. There can be no half-measures.'

It wasn't that Christine was personally lonely – she has tons of friends – but simply that family-wise she was totally alone. God had already set her in his eternal family and was now setting her into an earthly family.

So she became family to us. Jeremy, Nicholas and Elizabeth were delighted and sensed it really was from God. A short time later, she offered her resignation to the Bishop of Birmingham and came to work with Mary and me as Assistant Priest, totally unpaid yet commissioned for her new work in a lovely personal ceremony by the same bishop. Here was God's answer to our needs, so we could develop our emerging ministry. Isn't God good!

As Christine joined us, I reflected back on my uselessness at pastoral ministry. One of my early home communion visits with a very talkative ex-churchwarden of my new parish of St Boniface resulted in me falling asleep as she talked and talked and talked. I felt Christine was an answer to my personal weaknesses, as well as strength to Mary and me for the development of 'The Tour' and beyond.

In the meantime, Gaynor, although wonderfully rescued from her past, was still struggling. She was helping a new Christian called Saffron who had been part of the crowd of her old life, and it was raising all sorts of burried yet amazingly intense emotions within her . . .

20
Planting the Haven

You intended to harm me, but God intended it for good. (Genesis 50:20)

Gaynor was losing the plot. She was listening to her feelings, her needs and especially to that old crackle of excitement as her friend Saffron brought it all to a head.

They were walking arm in arm through the Bull Ring Centre when Saffron confided with an excitement tingling through her voice, 'Jackson's come back. Isn't that just amazing? You know how much I've been praying about him. Gaynor, honey, it's going to work this time, you wait and see. The Lord's going to work it out. I'm sure of it.'

Of course, Gaynor knew of Jackson from the many times she'd sat in the visitors' room as she'd supported Saffron visiting her 'beloved' in prison, and listened to emotive outpourings on the interminable journeys home.

As they sat in the fourth floor café overlooking the sparkling new concourse, Saffron told Gaynor how the newly released Jackson had swept her up into his arms again – just like the old days. The story unfolded of how she had said to him, 'But I'm a Christian now. Things are different from when you went inside.'

'No problem, sweet', Jackson had assured her. 'I really like the new spiritual you. I even went to see the chaplain in prison. In fact I was thinking of giving your church a go on Sunday. What do you think of that?'

'And why not, Gaynor?' she said earnestly. 'Maybe he really will make a fresh start, and stop all his violence and stuff. Maybe it was the lads and the drink that made him so vicious. Maybe it wasn't the real Jackson before.'

Saffron paused for a moment with the latte raised to her lips. 'Anyway, I'll tell you this Gaynor, he looked so good – and just the smell of him – good enough to eat; even good enough to . . .' She ended sharply with the feeling she was going too far, even for their warm friendship.

But for Gaynor it was pure torture. Not that Jackson was her type. It was just that the old life beckoned so enticingly. The ins and outs of relationships, the feeling of animal attraction and just doing her own thing, regardless. The text 'God will give you the desires of your heart' forced itself into the clamour of her mind. She felt strangely cheated as though somehow missing out.

Saffron was still in her own world. 'I told him, we can't just take up where we left off. Things are different now. "How so, sweet?" he commented. "After all, I do love you. Doesn't your Book say something about that? It can't be wrong if we love each other, can it?"'

She used her spoon to scoop up the milky foam round the cup rim. 'Perhaps, just perhaps, it'll work out. Maybe God is sorting it out for me.'

Gaynor thought in a flash of wistful thinking. 'Maybe he's speaking to me too. After all, I've got to have a life.'

* * *

Saffron rang Gaynor's mobile in the early hours. 'Jackson went out,' she sobbed, 'to sort a few things, he told me. He said, "Don't you worry, sweet. I'll be back soon enough. Not going to leave you again."' Saffron's voice changed to a lower, intimate pitch. 'That's what he said, but when he came back, I could tell he was really angry. He crashed up the stairs and flung the door open. "I'll bloody bible you," he yelled at me, Gaynor, for no reason at all. Then he just lashed out at me. Jackson's still Jackson, you see, Gaynor. Nothing's changed.' The sobbing intensified.

There were marks on Saffron as she met with Gaynor and another Christian friend the following day. The visible ones were to the upper arms. 'I told myself God was bringing us back together again,' she whimpered. 'I told myself that love was enough.'

God is love. Saffron was quite right in that part of her thinking. Yet God is also so much more than our often petty and careless human understanding of that misused and misunderstood word. The two friends took her to the local pub for a bar lunch.

'Saffron,' said Gaynor after she had listened to the story repeated quite a few times, 'God does speak. But don't you see? You were listening to everything but God. You were listening to what you wanted to hear.'

Their friend Claire cleared the little round table as a young man appeared with the food.

'Look how God spoke to Gaynor in the prison cell,' Claire reminded Saffron. 'That was clear enough, wasn't it?'

Saffron played with her salad. Quite a smoky salad by now judging from the number of cigarettes in the vicinity, but this was her home ground. A safe place for a bruised reed.

'I guess I knew really,' she put in slowly as she twisted the fork. 'I do know when Jesus speaks to me. It's just that . . .'

'Yea, I understand. Been there myself. Got the tee shirt,' commented Gaynor.

* * *

God is a speaking God. He speaks into situations, into people's lives and into churches, but he doesn't always say what we want to hear, nor does it necessarily correspond with our felt needs. It's listening to our speaking God that liberates the church from religious systems to be proactive, vibrant and exciting. Take the example of David and Helen Grist . . .

'New couple in church this morning,' I said to Mary. It's always exciting in an estate church when people just turn up. I continued, 'He's a teacher and she's a nurse, and they've just bought an ex-council house up the road. Real Christians by the look of how he was worshipping.'

'Do you mean Helen and David?' Mary retorted. 'The couple who have been coming for the last three weeks? Is that who you mean?'

'Oh.'

'They come from Kent and married some months ago,' smiled my competent spouse. 'And David was involved in the music down there. Did you know that?'

'Well, no . . .'

'And they want to get involved in things. Did they tell you?'

I surrendered. 'No. Nor do I know their life history or who they bank with or her mother's maiden name, but I suppose you do.'

Mary, in my opinion, just looked smug.

As they settled down, David's musical gifts and Helen's

excellent mothering of her new twins, James and Bethany, were a great joy within our growing fellowship. And it wasn't too long before they helped lead a week of mission at a failing inner-city church. Little did we know where it would lead.

After the successful mission, when I thought everything had settled down again, David came to see me. 'Wallace, I'm sure God has spoken to Helen and me.'

I groaned inwardly. Such a statement always means difficulty for me. What was he going to say?

'He wants us to leave St B's and go to that church where we did the mission. They need us, you see.'

Ministers hate losing members, even for such good and worthwhile reasons, so I tried some delaying tactics. 'But what about Helen being pregnant again? Is it the best time for her? Is this really what God wants?'

David looked at me with certainty in his eye. 'Yes, Wallace. We've heard from him, you see. It's what we must do.'

In a sort of historical, architectural way I loved their inner-city church. It had a vast, cobwebby splendour, with soaring walls and interesting looking balconies that weren't balconies. Of course, it had been erected as a Victorian statement of God.

David and Helen, ably 'assisted' by the twins, introduced us some while later to the small and elderly clique of well-wrapped-up people who appeared to herd together in a remote corner as far from the pulpit as possible. The area it served had ceased to be the white, churchgoing metropolis of better years. In fact the building stood as a memorial near interchanges, concrete 'things' and a new community housing project. The old had been swept away.

As we talked to the 'old guard', the twins played riotously around our feet and the new baby screamed vigorously.

'It feels right,' said David. 'I know it's right. It doesn't really make sense – to us or anybody – but it's what God is calling us to do.'

'But what about your children?' said Mary wistfully. 'What's going to happen to faith teaching for them?'

'Oh, I don't know,' responded Helen. 'But God must have an answer, don't you think? Otherwise he wouldn't be calling us to come here.' She sat with her arm linked with David's. 'I expect I'll end up doing Sunday school anyway. There's nobody else.'

'And we can keep our links with St B's.' David stood and walked across to the baby and picked her up. 'That way they can get the best of both worlds,' he announced bravely.

'But how do you know it's God?' I persisted, half of me anxious not to lose them from our growing fellowship and the other half concerned about their future. I suspect the former was more powerful.

'It's right,' David quietly replied as he rocked the baby. Helen nodded her own brave assent.

It certainly turned out to be right, but for the oddest of reasons. This lovely family worked for years in that failing church, running Sunday school, children's groups, teenagers and music; as well as occasionally helping to lead and preach. However, it was not a fellowship that listened to God, but rather one that sought to maintain what was and always had been. David and Helen had to learn the hard way to be humble servants and to empty themselves of pride and vanity. And to see, first hand, that the only way to be church led up the pathway of faith in a speaking God. All other ways are folly and nonsense, and lead, as in this case, to being declared redundant.

It is almost a picture for today's society: a redundant church building, slowly falling to pieces, in the midst of cars, clubs, industry and people; standing alone, separate, with a pitiful irrelevance.

However, under God's over-riding plan it turned out just right for this Christian couple. As the church was declared redundant, so they returned to St B's. It was with pleasure in one way, because they had many friends waiting to welcome them, but it was also in some confusion. As Helen plaintively asked me, 'I'm sure we got it right, but why has God allowed this to happen?'

I knew why. God had been shouting into our hearts for some years about our most deprived estate. It was separate because of a busy dual carriageway, but somehow it was separate spiritually too. It needed a gospel presence in its midst.

My curate, Martyn Saunders, was just the sort of dynamic person to spearhead the planting of a mission congregation, but it ached for longer term, humble, self-giving lay leadership. I felt sure that David and Helen, after their 'apprenticeship', would be God's people. It had been their preparation.

'Yes,' said David.

'Yes,' said Helen.

'They need a rest,' said some.

'Let them get their feet back under the table,' said others.

But the speaking God would have his way. It was time.

I stated one Sunday morning, 'I believe God has called us to plant a congregation at the school on the estate. David and Helen will become the leaders, but Martyn and Janette are going to kick-start it in their last year or so here. I'm calling on you, church, to go and do this.'

The rush was quite incredible. About a third of our congregation decided that it was right for them to go, along with the now swelling Grist family and Martyn and Janette

Saunders. They began to meet a few weeks later in our church hall Sunday by Sunday to prepare themselves. Then one Sunday off they went, and planted the congregation at the school on the estate, with David and Helen, plus children, at the fore.

Mary summed up the result. 'Isn't it interesting that many of the people whom the new congregation plant is reaching out towards have their roots in the parish area where David and Helen's church was declared redundant?' She was bubbling. 'Do you see? It's as if God declared the old building redundant, and so it was, but here is God's new building reaching the descendants of those who were brought out of those so-called slums to live here. Makes you think, doesn't it? It's as if David and Helen are God's continuum.'

'Hmmm,' I simply muttered. Yet she was right. Our God is a speaking God who sees the end from the beginning and stands beyond, yet in the very midst. 'Yes, it's very God,' I confirmed with a growing excitement.

Some years later, the Haven congregation is living and thriving. It has its own identity and is not a clone of St B's. It was a plant succoured in the call of God within people's hearts and minds. It came into being because God is a speaking God and some people were willing to listen and act.

But planting the new congregation hasn't been without its difficulties and sacrifices.

'You've given yourself a nightmare. You know that, don't you?' Mary likes to make straightforward comments, but this one took me totally by surprise.

'Excuse me?'

Mary threw another illegal crumb to the gulls that wheeled overhead as we sat beside the harbour in the lovely Northumberland fishing village of Seahouses.

'Two things really. You are starting up a lay-led church plant and you know the problems that will cause. It just won't fit in with the system. It's all clergy this and clergy that in the Church of England. What about communion, for instance? And what if they don't do things your way? Or rebel against the Anglican way? Why do you think there are so few lay-led congregations? Do you think you are the first with this idea?'

'Haven't you seen the notice about not feeding the sea-gulls, Mary? It just makes them into scavengers.' I had to get my word in because I felt attacked. 'Anyway, the boat is loading up now.'

The boat left for a scenic tour of the Farne Islands, even stopping for a quick landing at the Longshore Lighthouse before giving us an hour to enjoy the National Trust quiet-ness of the Inner Farne. I remembered how, years ago, my father had been divebombed by one of the birds during the nesting season.

As we returned to the mainland and sat in the harbour café, I foolishly asked, 'And the second problem?'

'St B's. Or Lighthouse as we call it now. It will feel really different. You've lost a lot of the "keenies" to Haven and it will no longer feel full and vibrant and successful. I know you. You really like to come out to a full church every Sunday – and it won't be. It'll be like turning the clock back. You'll see.'

'No way, José,' I spluttered with laughter. 'You're just being a fuddy-duddy.'

'Well, maybe. Let's wait and see.' Mary emptied her coffee cup with an air of finality.

* * *

Of course, and annoyingly, she was absolutely right. Haven is exciting but full of the problems of growth as it struggles out of the confines of slavery to the system. It has people with different ideas in leadership – people who do not necessarily conform to Anglican norms. Every week new issues arise and need to be battled with, and the vicar's word is no longer the be all and end all. After all, leadership has been given to others; certainly under authority but not under domination.

Yet I love the new mission, because I see God working in the problems as the gospel is being made accessible to the estate. How difficult that would have been if we had adhered to the traditional model of church. Also I profoundly believe in the royal priesthood being the church from top to toe. It is something to fight for within the context of God-given leadership.

And Mary was right about the cost to Lighthouse as the effect of many 'keenies' moving on to start the Haven was felt. The first Sunday afterwards, it was an entirely different place. It was as if we were at the bottom of the slope again, as the sheer cost of being a different church hit us between the eyes. I realised how comfortable we had all become, sinking back into enjoying our worship and feeling as though we had arrived rather than being proactive in our faith adventure.

God had initiated the Haven through David and Helen, but he still had much to teach us about being a proactive mission congregation . . .

21
They Devoted Themselves . . .

> They devoted themselves to the apostles' teaching and to the fellowship, to the breaking of bread and to prayer. (Acts 2:42)

Mary first gave her life to Jesus at the kitchen sink!

'As I was standing there, looking out onto the garden,' she remembers, 'I was overcome with a sense of the rightness of the gospel. Somehow it all made absolute sense in my mind, and I knew it was the moment. And it all seemed to match in with the beauty of nature as I gazed out with my hands in the washing-up bowl.'

Often I hear her go on to say, 'I didn't really feel any different. There was no great power surge or anything. Just an absolute sense of rightness. It was quite a few weeks later that I perceived the Lord in a physical way. I remember quietly praying one night in the sitting room when Wallace was working late. And I felt a gentle warm breeze flow over my face, and, at the same time, a sense of something like feathers caressing me. It was just . . . supernatural, and absolutely beautiful.' She continues the story, 'And I found I was beginning to speak in tongues. The words simply formed somewhere in my spirit and came out of my mouth, and I felt so at one with Jesus.'

It is Mary's encounter with Jesus and his Spirit that has led to her being filled with passion about ministry and excited about sharing her faith. Most of the now depleted Lighthouse congregation felt the same as her, with a desire to serve the Lord, yet a cruel spiritual apathy had come upon us. It was something to do with a different spiritual dynamic, as many of our committed members had left to start the Haven, and something to do with feeling superior (we were a church that had made it, and we had forgotten our roots of humble and loving application in the power of the Servant King). The church had lost its sparkle and dynamism, and had fallen into the trap of maintenance Christianity. It is a truism that such a state dramatically affects the ongoing, underlying mission of the church. We can do all the right things and run all the correct systems and methods, but unless it is underpinned by active love of Jesus, it all comes to nought. We knew the issue, an issue shared with many fellowships, but not the answer.

* * *

Jock had us all in fits of laughter. His quick-witted mind and breakneck speed of tongue combined to make witty comment on life, with vicars in particular taking the brunt. I commented back, in the words of my mother from early years, 'Jock, you are so sharp you must have swallowed razor blades for breakfast.'

This was a mistake, because everyone then had their own silly sayings or old wives' tales to contribute: 'Born in Sheffield he was,' as well as the inevitable misquote,

'Sharpest knife in the drawer, he is.' But sometimes it's good to be light-hearted at serious moments, otherwise it all gets too intense.

'OK, enough of this hilarity. Let's get down to it,' responded Martin Knox. 'Let's spend time together with God and see what he is saying to us and the church. We know the problem, so let's get to it.' Then he added, 'I know God will show us what to do about it. It's his church, and his heart is to make it zing. That's right, isn't it?'

We were at the start of a weekend away with a smallish leadership group to hear God about how to deal with the spiritual apathy that we discerned was becoming a real issue at St B's Lighthouse congregation.

'You are right, Martin,' I commented, taking charge. 'So let's start with God's word and prayer.'

After 30 minutes or so of Bible study and spoken prayers, I went on, 'So let's do what Martin said and spend time listening to God. We'll spend about 90 minutes in quiet, each of us asking God the question, 'In what direction do you want us to lead St B's?' Then we'll come back together again. Sit here if you want to, or have a wander or whatever is right for you. But let's give this time to God to speak to us, rather than us prattling on at him.'

I went off for a gentle stroll through the spring countryside. I find it so easy to listen to God while walking, but quite difficult if I just sit there. Others stayed in their chairs and Martin stretched out on his bed.

One and a half hours later, we met up again, coffee brewing and notebooks in hand.

'You vicars get paid for this, you know,' Jock told me with a smile. 'Paid to pray. I don't know. Even paid to go to church. Mind you, most of you need it, judging by the state of some of your churches.'

'Jock, that's absolutely outrageous,' glared his wife Sheena in false shock.

How awesome and astonishing was the result of that time of listening. Each one of us came back with the same concept, fed by different scriptures, pictures and thoughts according to our individual personalities. But the sum total was the word 'devotion' and the passage 'They devoted themselves to the apostles' teaching and to the fellowship, to the breaking of bread and to prayer'.[1] Amazing. And isn't it awesome how God can speak to his people when we give him time, space and an enquiring mind? He even gave us a couple of key worship songs.

Over the next year, the Sunday preaching and overall dynamic of the church was fed by the biblical expression of devotion, focusing, as the scripture said, on teaching, fellowship, breaking of bread and prayer. Again we had to break free of the prescribed system of themes and readings. The lectionary is good, but often the good can be an enemy of the best for a particular set of circumstances. The hub of the devotion theme was a series of new devotion evenings, where we simply worshipped and allowed spiritual gifts to flourish in a gentle, safe, organised yet laid-back environment.

* * *

One of our young folk, Rose Hudson, was specially caught up by this devotion to the Lord on a particularly lovely evening of sung worship, which we shared with an estate fellowship from Manchester. Through a spiritual gift from the

[1] Acts 2:42.

Lord, she shared a picture she had been given during that 'devoted' time of the need for their fellowship to be like a castle against the devilish probes of the evil one. Rose shared the poignant reading from 1 Peter 5:8: 'Your enemy the devil prowls about like a roaring lion looking for someone to devour.' The truth and reality of this word of knowledge, coupled with the Scripture reading, was totally evident from the faces of our visitors. It obviously touched a vital strand within their situation, even though Rose knew nothing whatsoever about them.

Our visitors agreed to form a circle and hold hands in front of the Lord's table to symbolise a castle of unity and strength in the Lord. Then, one by one, our folk anointed their folk with oil in the name of the Father, the Son and the Holy Spirit as well as praying for their protection and firm foundation in Jesus.

It was such a wonderful, heartwarming spiritual moment, and it had arisen out of spiritual listening to God a year previously, taking note of the wisdom he gave us and acting upon it as we met in devotion before his throne, and then Rose offering to be vulnerable with her spiritual gift and speaking what truly turned out to be God's word.

Being devoted to God means exercising the gifts of the Spirit. This is so clearly marked out in the earthly life of Jesus himself. Looking at the classic list of spiritual gifts in 1 Corinthians 12:1f, we see the ministry of our Lord laid out: healings, discernment, knowledge, wisdom, prophecy and so on. All except, perhaps, speaking in tongues. We don't really know about that one.

Of course, we have our fair share of 'odd' words, with some people sharing quite weird understandings and others allowing personal agendas to rise to the surface. But it has always been like this and doesn't form any reason for locking up spiritual gifts as potentially divisive and problematic. Indeed, if the early church had taken this 'safe' option, the whole of the outpouring of the Christian faith would have been totally curtailed. Often I refer to the story of the early church in the Acts of the Apostles as 'acts of the Holy Spirit' – as do many other people. The church has always been in the business of testing things out to avoid wrong doctrine, excesses and the ways of evil people. The voice of God is absolute truth. It is a voice totally in line with Scripture. It is a voice that can be tested out. It is a voice that booms through history to reach his children of today.

Jesus said, 'I will build my church, and the gates of hell will not overcome it'[2] and the fellowship that fails to hear the speaking God through the spiritual giftings of its people, fails in fundamental discipleship and allows the dough mountain of the system to dominate against the living seeds of proactive faith through the grace of Jesus Christ.

Of course, the dough mountain of the ecclesiastical system has trouble with spiritual gifts because they upset the status quo. They take away from the simplicity of liturgical uniformity and plunge the establishment into destabilising questioning. Is God really speaking? How can 'pew' Christians, who are sometimes seen as mere punters, hear from God and discern his prophetic direction for a church? And what if it should happen, shock/horror, in the midst of a service of worship?

For Mary, speaking in tongues was and is a gift that God gave her as an individual Christian, yet it is also something to be exercised, with the other gifts, in the wider body of Christ. Of course, she had to stand alone with God as she spoke this spiritual language, yet the whole life of a church

---

[2] Matthew 16:18.

develops through that individual spirituality of its members. Fruit of the Spirit[3] coupled with gifts of the Spirit make a powerful contribution to a church where people love the Lord. Give me a church that loves the Lord and I will show you one with a dynamically outward spirit of mission.

The church that wants to move the dough mountain of ecclesiastical systems and rely on the faith dynamic must embrace spiritual fruit and practise spiritual gifts, and be prepared to buck a system that would tie Christians up in the chains of how it has always been . . .

[3] Galatians 5:22.

22

'An Angel Spoke to You?'

Now an angel of the Lord said to Philip . . . (Acts 8:26)

The thing about listening to God is that it leads to the most outrageous and exciting situations, whereas slavishly conforming to the religious system signs the death warrant of proactive, New Testament Christianity.

Philip was a man who had the early church at his fingertips. The crowds had heard him preach with amazing authority and seen the miraculous signs he did. No doubt he was the man to take the church forward in Samaria and beyond, especially after he'd successfully led Simon the Sorcerer to repentance. Philip could become, perhaps, one of the founding elders of the Christian church. Until the angel spoke God's word to him: 'Go south to the road – the desert road – that goes down from Jerusalem to Gaza.'[1]

Maybe the others, like Peter and John, said to him, 'Come on, Phil, sort yourself out. Your ministry is just opening up in Samaria – all these converts to nurture and our new church to organise. What's going to happen to them if you go gallivanting off? Have you thought this through properly?'

You can imagine Philip just looking at them and saying,

[1] Acts 8:26.

'It's what I have to do. It's what God wants. You should know his voice if anybody does.'

So Philip, with the Spirit's leading, had this amazing meeting with the Ethiopian eunuch, and after a shortish time of teaching him about Jesus, Philip baptised him.

Today's church would be astonished:

'Philip, you say an angel spoke to you?'

'Philip, you baptised him without doing the preparation course?'

And if he was an Anglican: 'Philip, you baptised him without the bishop's permission and without confirmation?'

'Philip, you say the Spirit suddenly took you away?'

The church needs a system – of course it does – but the system is there to serve not to be the master. We need to offer accessible doorways to spirituality which are not barricaded by traditional expectations.

We discovered that the same dynamic of the Holy Spirit's calling to Philip was needed for Liam, our modern-day seeker who really wanted to discover Jesus for himself. Trouble was, his brain was addled. He'd been taking too much heroin for far too long. Liam couldn't think straight. His mind no longer grasped concepts. He was on the slope to user oblivion. Then Liam got religion. Not faith and joy in Jesus, but almost some sort of religious mania. The heroin stuff got intermingled with religious stuff and Liam was in a black hole somewhere in the middle.

'Vicar?' he questioned, as we first met. 'How can I be forgiven? I've committed the unforgivable sin.'

He had walked off the council estate street into St Boniface Church – a thin streak of a young man with a pinched face and a ragged T-shirt hanging off his skeleton frame. Liam looked earnestly at me for a complete reply that would sort out everything.

'What do you mean, unforgivable sin?' I answered defensively, not having a clue how to deal with such a question. And anyway, the pupils of his eyes were pinpricks, suggesting other issues. He looked like a little lost soul.

Liam was a child of the estate. I quickly learned his sad history and his even sadder present circumstances. Later I took him to his hostel room with its four plain walls, bed and nothing else, except dirty cups, plates and bottles. He'd been introduced to his 'stuff of life' quite a few years earlier by a friend's mother, and that had been the beginning of the end.

'Liam, there is no way you have committed the unforgivable sin,' I and others insisted on many occasions as he asked the same question again and again to everyone he met around the church.

Jim sat for hours with him, telling the story of how Jesus had rescued him from his suicide bid on the M5,[2] and others befriended him by gradually integrating Liam into the small fellowship of daytime users of the church building. But the heroin would have its way and Liam's addled brain just couldn't take it in. A lost soul indeed. Whatever was the way forward for him?

'Have you been baptised?' I asked him thoughtfully one day.

'No,' he said. 'What does "baptised" mean?'

'Christened – you know.'

'Don't think so. Why?'

'Liam, you've already said sorry and asked Jesus into your heart. Do you remember?'

He looked vague.

'Well, baptism is where you stand up and tell everyone that you've done that, then I pour water all over you to show your

[2] See *Angels on the Walls*.

sins have been washed away. Just like Jesus told us to do,' I said firmly.

'I'd love to do that,' replied the unhappy young man. 'Can we do it soon?' Of course he would have forgotten the whole conversation by the next day.

I forgot about the conversation as well – until some weeks later, when God spoke to me so clearly and profoundly during a time of prayer. I had that absolute sense within me that is so difficult to put into words, that baptism was totally important for Liam. It was a word of knowledge, I suppose, that the Spirit put into my heart and just had to be acted upon.

I shared my word with the churchwarden. 'Nic, we have to do this. I believe it's what the Spirit requires of us – just to get on with it, never mind all the churchy stuff. So let's just do it. Now. Tomorrow morning during the service.' Normally we would prepare people very carefully and link it with confirmation. That's the Anglican way.

'Brilliant,' agreed Nic. 'If there's one thing Liam needs it's cleansing from the past and from heroin, and to be put right with Jesus. I'll get the paddling pool ready.'

Come 9.30 am, I hammered on the hostel door. An untidy, braless young girl with a silver ring jutting from her lower lip admitted the dog collar after a short display of attitude. I went upstairs to Liam's room and there he was, sleeping off last night's excesses.

'Come on, Liam. Let's go. You're being baptised this morning.'

'Baptised? What does that mean?' Liam said in a rerun of our previous conversation, which he had completely forgotten. But he was absolutely delighted when he cottoned on. I saw the smile reach his eyes.

It was a great morning. We poured gallons of water over Liam as he stood in the paddling pool beside the font. 'I baptise you, Liam, in the name of the Father, the Son and the Holy Spirit.' He just glowed, as did the whole congregation. An outstanding presence of the Lord just seized the church family as we rejoiced with Liam. 'And, Lord, break the habit. Break it this morning. Get rid of Liam's need for the heroin,' prayed one person after another. What a morning of sheer grace, coming out of listening to God as we bucked the religious system and just got to grips with Liam's needs.

Liam came off heroin that morning. Since then he has grown deeply. His brain is still slightly addled, as he would be the first to agree, but with the habit broken he is beginning to emerge as a changed young man. He's attended our Christian foundations course four times over, and each time he gets more and more in touch with faith things. Even the inevitable 'How can I be forgiven? I've committed the unforgivable sin?' has become less inevitable.

One thing Liam does know is the gospel. He has joined outreach teams to share his new faith and tells vividly of how Jesus is saving him. What a Saviour we have in Jesus!

The enemy enshrouds many things with cobwebs, layers of deceit and strands of lies. The system of church often imposes hoops to jump through that favour the strong rather than empower the weak; it keeps control and tends towards ultra-conservative domination. But Jesus stands among us and says, 'I am among you as one who serves.'[3] His service ended on the cross of Calvary as he gave his life for us.

Philip, as far as we know, served as an evangelist and equipped his four daughters, and no doubt many others, to take the church forward in faith. James, his contemporary and the leader of the early church, left awesome scriptural teaching for following generations about seeking the Lord's

---

[3] Luke 22:27.

will and not merely making up your own mind.[4] His selfless devotion, according to the Jewish historian Josephus, led to the Lord's brother being stoned to death in AD 62. Another fellow worker, Peter, became known after his death as the honorary first Bishop of Rome; without a bishop's 'palace'! It is probable that he was martyred in Rome during the AD 64 persecution of Christians. I often wonder what happened to Peter's wife. Was she left to help lead the growing church? We know little detail about those who rose up to lead the church forward after those giants of faith.

Established leaders need to teach the rising leaders to listen to God and proactively offer liberty as well as wisdom to equip the new generation for a faith ministry. As church leaders, we have to beware of becoming enmeshed in the system and allowing the reactionary tendencies of age to stultify God's church. We are called to give guidance and freedom to that continual renewing movement of the Holy Spirit within a framework that supports and strengthens. It is a risky business releasing young Christians to express faith in accessible up-to-date ways, and allowing the shackles of control to be questioned. For too long the church has been oppressive rather than freeing, holding on to the past as if we have somehow got it right, whereas the story of history is that we have often got it horribly and sadly wrong.

I desire to see a church that gives form, substance and safety through adhering strongly to revealed Christian truth, yet offers joy, celebration and liberation for new generations to seek and find and to discover afresh for themselves that God is good!

Yet how strongly we hold on to the past, and how easy it is to make church inaccessible to those who are not of our ilk . . .

---

[4] James 4:15.

23
Jumping through Hoops

> You shut the kingdom of heaven in men's faces . . . nor will you let those enter who are trying to. (Matthew 23:13)

The vagrant stumbled through the open church doorway one Tuesday morning, right in the middle of our prayers. He tottered up to our prayer table, unshaven whiskers bristling, coat tied together with string, a possessions bag firmly gripped under his right arm and a ripe aura of stale alcohol, cigarettes and dirt.

'I want some food,' he slowly enunciated, with the authority of the drunk, and promptly collapsed on the edge of a vacant chair, but mostly on the floor.

Jim looked at him, then looked at me, then back at our unexpected visitor, then with a wry smile hauled him onto the chair. 'I guess that's the end of prayers this morning. I wonder who he is. Anyone ever seen him before?'

'An angel I would guess,' said someone with attempted humour. 'Jim, you know what the good book says about ministering to angels without knowing it.[1] Looks as if God has sent you one.'

---

[1] Hebrews 13:2.

'Perhaps he has,' replied Jim knowingly as he took a tissue and wiped the now-gaping mouth of the anonymous sleeper.

George became a friend and a handful. Especially for Jim. And slowly his terrible story emerged.

'He was a professional soldier, you know,' Jim informed me one day. 'Trained for the SAS, or so he says, and became a sniper. Over his early years he killed man after man in cold blood through the sights of his rifle, but it slowly killed him inside as well. He just cannot live with himself and his memories.' Jim paused thoughtfully. 'His wife's left him and his children ignore him. Wallace, he's just a shell.'

Jim felt the power of George's need and, in some quiet way, began to love him, even though he often remarked, with a woe-filled expression, 'That guy will drive me round the bend one day.' Indeed, it was Jim's 'love in Jesus' of our vagrant 'angel' that helped the church fellowship to see George as a gift rather than a liability. Isn't it a shocking thing that our natural minds can turn people into problems, and that, so often, the church bows to those fallen natural feelings rather than seizing the opportunity to welcome the stranger?

As the months turned into years, our unexpected visitor quietly began to take communion. I often walked to the easy chair at the back of the church which had become his, to give him prayer and the bread and wine. And just as quietly, George began to make sense of faith in Jesus Christ.

At much the same time we were seeking to welcome another 'angel'. My first memory of Jolene was that of a person robbed of her selfhood. I'd spotted her many times continually and pointlessly wandering the streets of the estate. Her emaciated body was enshrouded in shapeless clothes of garish colours. The amateurishly applied lipstick, together with totally inappropriate high heels and skimpy skirt, gave the vague impression of a prostitute. After Jolene first stepped though the doors, she sat with head shrunken into herself, as if she felt she were of no value.

'Good morning,' I ventured.

Jolene hardly replied.

'Brilliant to see you here,' I added. This was followed by an uncomfortable silence, until I made an excuse to wander off to speak to someone else.

This scenario was repeated week after week, with the one exception when she said, without looking at me, 'Vicar, I need some stuff for my new baby – some food and nappies and things, like. Can you help me?'

'Baby?' I offered back. 'I haven't seen your baby yet.'

'I have to go to hospital soon, to have it, like,' she replied after a pause.

'Yes, of course we can help. Just as soon as it happens. No problem.' I had my doubts though: it all seemed so artificial.

Time spilled by, and sure enough the pregnancy was forgotten about, but she suddenly had to go to hospital for a major operation – or so she said.

Jolene began to come to everything, with a new story every time; it seemed she couldn't get enough attention. However, I was deeply encouraged as she began to respond to holy communion. I always use the words 'We welcome all who love the Lord to join us at his table this morning' and she obviously took me at my word and did exactly that.

Later, the complexities of Jolene's background emerged: violence, alcohol abuse and powerful, manipulative relatives forcing her to 'tell stories' – right from childhood – to gain more and more benefits from the authorities. Her important step of faith was simply to come to the Lord's table and receive of Jesus. How this fitted in with evangelical conversion, I did not then know, and it was all too complex to put into a simple formula. The great thing was that Jolene, in the midst of all sorts of complex self-myths and deception, was somehow responding to the Lord.

The big BUT with both Jolene and George was that one was not baptised and neither one was a confirmed member of the Anglican church. Jolene's baptism had been an excuse for a booze-up by her family when she was a baby and in no way reflected faith, except maybe that of the baptising vicar. The Church of England demands baptism and confirmation before receiving the bread and wine, and this almost demands 'jumping through hoops' for the Georges and Jolenes of this world in order for them to conform to the way we do things. So what should I do? Did I have to put law before grace? Or did my own actions in inviting 'all who love the Lord' bring on the dilemma in the first place? Yet people are more important than institutions and their rules. Jesus surely demonstrated that to be true.

I never did bring George to baptism or confirmation. He had a good if childish faith, but then didn't Jesus delight in such an attitude? Frankly, George couldn't cope with the outward ways of religion, but he could sit in his easy chair and receive Jesus in the sacrament. And, at the same time, we had deep talks about his past with a real, if not churchy, repentance. This very week I am preparing for his funeral, and I can say with all honesty that although George was far from a good churchman, somewhere inside him I perceived he had come to love Jesus. And that's enough. His Saviour will be opening the great doors, and George will know peace and comfort at last.

Jolene, however, has delighted the church fellowship by reaffirming the 'boozy' baptism vows of her childhood in a very watery ceremony, which would lead, a few months later, to confirmation.

* * *

The assistant bishop was not happy. 'You shouldn't have done that, you know.' He looked at me severely. 'What do you mean, "re-affirm baptism vows with full immersion" anyway? She's already baptised and that's it. You shouldn't have done it,' he repeated. 'And if you did, it should have been with permission and at confirmation.'

We were in the vestry of St John's Church in Harborne, a well-to-do and excellent evangelical church.

'How can you say that?' I argued, getting slightly red in the face. 'Look at what Jolene has been through in her life.' I couldn't tell him the details because of confidentiality, but it was obvious that here was a woman with a past. 'Jolene was desperate to have all her past washed off her – all the deceit and abuse and obvious sins – and she just couldn't see any reality in her infant baptism because she continually heard her family bragging of a great booze-up to wet the baby's head.'

I went on getting more and more worked up: 'You see, Jolene just wanted it done properly and have all the horrible parts of her past washed away. That's what she wanted.'

'How did you do it, anyway?' he persisted. I think he half-wanted to agree, but the weight of Anglican tradition was on his shoulders.

'We hired a birthing pool,' I smiled at him. 'Apt, don't you think? Instead of midwives and a baby being born, Jolene testified to being reborn of the Spirit and I just got in there with her and re-affirmed her baptism with water. It was brilliant.'

The vestry door opened and a churchwarden appeared. 'Time to get started,' he said. The assistant bishop and I managed to exchange a smile and a prayer.

'I confirm you in the name of the Father, Son and Holy Spirit,' said the bishop to Jolene. I was really blessed as quite a large number of our folk confirmed their faith in the Lord Jesus Christ and their joy in being welcomed into the church of God.

The story did not end there. A minor crisis had arisen during the preceding week. Rhys, a young man from a poor home, had been nominated by the confirmation group to come and see me. He said, 'You know at the rehearsal? They told us to wear our best clothes and not to forget to polish our shoes. What should we do?'

The problem was obvious to anyone who lives on the estates. Rhys had no shoes, polished or otherwise. Cheap trainers with untied laces were his only footwear and 'best clothes' were, for him, an alien historical concept from another century.

Rhys went on, 'And did you know that we have to process and have name cards so the bishop knows who we are? And you wouldn't believe how Ruby is just shivering with anxiety about it all.'

The Church of England loves special events. It reverts immediately to organisation and pomp and traditional ways. And it does it all extremely well. We excel in full, complicated liturgy, wordy hymns, chanting, small print booklets, complicated instructions and choreographed movement. And we do it all with a churchy perspective that if it isn't done perfectly, then we are in some way offending God; that the worship is less than acceptable to the Lord. But experience has taught me that such a format misses the mark as far as people like Jolene, Rhys and others are concerned.

I rang the vicar of St John's. We are good friends and we admire each other's calling to different types of community. Canon John Hughes is an exceptional priest, who excels in his sphere.

'John, we have a problem here,' I softly suggested, and went on to explain Rhys's worries and the group's unhappiness.

John reacted immediately and altered all that was in his power to do so. We both discovered that what was right and good and proper for his middle-class parish was equally unsuitable for our folk. The establishment of the church has ways of doing things, with rules and regulations set down, and clearly we need order and decency in our proceedings. But the question raised through George and Jolene and many others is this: does the organisation of the church exist for the church's sake or the people's sake? And have 'religion-loving' people hijacked things and held them to the detriment of our postmodern generation? Has the institution become greater than its purpose and goal?

For many people of this generation, the institutional church is seen as a medieval bastion of establishment sitting on the fringe of society and, perhaps more surprisingly, on the margins of God himself. It is suitable for 'religious' people but inapplicable to the man, woman or child on the street.

And to some extent they are right. The Spirit of God is surely calling us to make the church accessible to all – a strong tower of God with ever open doors rather than a barricaded castle of middle-England religion. How easy it is to unthinkingly 'shut the kingdom of heaven in men's faces'.[2]

A great evangelist of my generation, Canon David

[2] Matthew 23:13.

Watson, offered a serious warning that the church system was erecting a barrier around the person of Jesus. Today you and I are witnessing Canon Watson's largely unheeded prophetic insight of the 1970s bearing a terrible fruit in our postmodern beginnings of the twenty-first century. Let us, together, take note that the future church may return to its calling to be accessible, full of faith and sensitively responsive to the needs of the very diverse communities we are called to serve, because we know that the eternal plan is that 'God our Saviour . . . wants all men to be saved and to come to a knowledge of the truth'.[3]

To take a church forward prophetically, the leaders often have to be hard-nosed and ready for confrontation with the old ways. One great writer said that the propensity of dust is to settle. Similarly, the propensity of the church is to get set in its ways unless we take action as Jesus himself showed us, and as national tragedies bring to light . . .

[3] 1 Timothy 2:3–4.

24

What Would Jesus Do?

God is spirit, and his worshippers must worship in spirit and in truth. (John 4:24)

The woman was hot and bothered. It had been a long walk to the village well, and she felt distinctly irritated. When she arrived, a stranger was looking towards her. 'Who does he think he is?' she muttered under her breath. She ignored him and went about her task.

'Will you give me a drink?' asked the man.

Again she ignored him. After all, he was clearly not of her people. Yet there was something about him that touched her in a way that she couldn't even begin to understand.

'Will you give me a drink?' he repeated – not arrogantly as most men would have done, but with a humble strength she had rarely witnessed before.

'You are a Jew,' she replied after some hesitation, 'and I am a Samaritan woman.' Everybody knew that Jews held themselves above Samaritans. What was this guy thinking of?

Then he started, out of the blue, to talk about God – something about living water.[1] But she liked him, there was something about him, so she started to talk, and the words

[1] John 4:10.

just flowed. To her, God was just religion – something that happened at the special hill altars; the men doing religious things. She knew the Jews had a thing about Jerusalem. You could only worship God at that temple of theirs, and only in their weird ways. What did she care? But she liked this man, so she used her pitcher to offer him some water from the cool depths of the well.

But then again, there was this spooky understanding he had. Somehow he knew all about her; knew she'd been married five times and was living with a new man.

He was talking again: 'A time is coming . . . when the true worshippers will worship the Father in spirit and truth.' Funny, he wasn't talking about 'doing' religion but about God as Father, and worship as something, well . . . spiritual! She was gob-smacked.

* * *

True worship is in spirit and in truth. Jesus said so, so it must be true. I've been to high churches where they have offered truly spiritual worship. I've been to charismatic gatherings where powerful worship has filled the meeting place with electricity. I've been to liturgical services that were full of worship. I've been to school halls, decorated orthodox chapels, gymnasiums, sports centres and gothic buildings where true worship has rung from the rafters.

I've also been to places similar to all the above where worship has been turgid, monotonous and flat. True worship is not about building or denomination or style or music or anything earthly like that. It's about spirit and truth. It's about Jesus.

The grandson of the famous Old Testament priest, Eli, was called Ichabod, meaning 'the glory of the Lord has departed'. Worship was nothing without the ark of the covenant, which told of God's presence among his people. Once the ark was gone, the glory had gone. In our churches today, once religion takes over from faith, the glory is on its way out. 'Worship' becomes an empty shell as people go through the ritual. 'Ichabod' is a fearsome reality of a church that does not move in the power of the Holy Spirit. It's part of our learning process to make church worship authentic, relevant and even topical. Take one difficult Sunday a few years ago . . .

'I just can't believe it. How dreadful,' I muttered to myself as I rose from the kitchen bench. 'It just can't be true,' I reiterated to the radio as I walked across to turn the volume up.

There are some world events that stand out in your memory. They almost freeze the moment. The murder of John F. Kennedy, the famous first words from the moon, and now another such moment: the tragic death of Princess Diana in the Paris subway.

It was early Sunday morning and the vicarage was waking ready for our 'working day'. On a sort of automatic pilot, I made a cup of tea and took it upstairs. 'You aren't going to believe this,' I said to a waking Mary as I handed it to her and broke the news. Even between us there was a sort of stunned silence and we had to go downstairs to recheck the reality.

'Well, what are you going to do?' questioned my wife. I noticed the 'you' rather than a 'we', realising she was starting to think about the service looming ahead in just over an hour. My carefully prepared sermon was ready on scraps of paper and in my head, but as I glanced at my overhead visuals they appeared almost mocking in that they did not address the topic that would be on everybody's mind in the immediate aftermath of Diana's tragic car smash. What should I do? All my training and past screamed at me to continue as normal and merely to mention the death in our intercessions and pray for her children. In this way the liturgy and sermon could continue, like a ship ploughing on through stormy seas regardless of the elements. That was the system, and the system of religion was deeply rooted in my training and subconscious.

WWJD (What Would Jesus Do) said the wristband on one of the young people as we met for pre-service prayers. My eyes narrowed. Well, what *would* Jesus do? I decided he would most certainly react to the people and their needs, and the system would take second place. And it was clear from reactions amid those praying that everyone was quite shocked.

The service started in a muted atmosphere. Some had not heard the news until they arrived at church. As far as I could see, everybody was preoccupied with the unfolding event of the morning. After welcoming people, I took my sermon papers out of my pocket and tore them up – much to the delight of all the children and young people. And then, as a Christian community, we began to speak and share together about the situation. People of all ages, including children, came to the front and prayed as we voiced our grief and considered our Christian response. Why should such a thing happen? Why does God allow tragedies? Our musicians chose and led us in appropriate worship songs and hymns. Together we shared the moment.

A few years later we were to react in much the same way to the terrible terrorist attacks on New York and Washington. On the very same Tuesday night we had a carefully planned praise and teaching meeting that was similarly turned upside down to meet the new circumstances. What good is the best church programme if it is not touching where people are hurting? A week after the shocking event, it was our Harvest Festival, but how could we sing 'We plough the fields and scatter', seemingly referring back to a rustic England of happy years, when the words 'WAR ON TERRORISM' dominated our thoughts and imaginations? (Anyway, I've never ploughed a field, and the only seeds I've ever scattered were mustard and cress seeds, in my childhood, on blotting paper!)

It's difficult to abandon the set ways. As a leader one waits for the inevitable criticism from some; after all, it's quite impossible to get it right for everybody. Yet God's Spirit seems to be blessing so many churches that step out of the ordinary into the faith dynamic. The only way to move the barricade of ordinariness is through the dynamic of spiritual faith and spiritual worship – stepping out into God.

Dynamic, prayerful, authentic worship appears to be the key to any church moving on in vitality and growth. I hear and read of the wonderful prayer mountain of a Korean church, which inputs amazing spirituality into church life. The house church movement in China, after decades of persecution, has been revealed as awesomely massive and vigorous, not in the sense of ritual and establishment, but of thousands, perhaps millions, of people meeting Christ through simple, biblical faith, expressed in deep-felt worship. East and West, as well as the developing world, tell us of great movements of God's Spirit. So the opportunity to fly to North America was like a dream come true for Mary and me . . .

* * *

It looked so good from out of the blue sky – the Golden Gate Bridge guarding San Francisco. The long economy class flight was nearing its end and there was California stretched below us.

I had written to the Cathedral of Faith in San Jose, building on some tenuous connections and asking if Mary and I could stay with and learn from them for a few weeks. A church secretary had written back and offered to open up her home to this English vicar. Amazingly, she and her husband subsequently learned that they had to fly to London for his business at exactly the same time, so they decided to make a holiday out of it.

'Well, I have a vicarage if you would like to borrow it,' I commented, wondering how I could explain council estate culture to a family from the edge of Silicon Valley. But no, they were on expenses!

'Honey, just use our house, won't you? It's for Jesus, isn't it?' So we ended up in a wonderful, middle-class, stereotypical American home free of charge for three weeks. Isn't God good?

'Water the lawn, would you? But don't cut it. The firm does that and they get annoyed.' The lovely American accent flowed over us as Courtney added, 'And water any house plants you see looking a bit brown.' Chuck took me on a tour of his massive 'gar-ahge'. I almost needed a compass to find my way back to the kitchen door.

The following Sunday, I took the 'Bible belt' freeway to the incredible Cathedral of Faith. The mammoth car park looked rather like the Sheffield shopping centre I'd seen from the motorway some months before, but it was *full* of the cars of people who had come to praise the Lord. My spirit soared. If only it could be like this in England! If only churches could blossom in faith! If only the Spirit would move over rainy Manchester like he had over sunny California! As Mary and I sat on the platform before the thousands of praising Christians, I felt so weird. Little did they know that their 'Anglican vicar' pastored a flock that would hardly have filled their ante-room, let alone this plush-seated, close-carpeted auditorium of God.

No doubt they had all sorts of issues, and the USA is far from 'God's own country', yet I felt so profoundly and deliciously encouraged – certainly by Courtney and Chuck's personal generosity, but mostly by the sheer omnipotent, awesome sense of God; that he is at work all over the globe, calling people of all colours and all nations to worship in spirit and in truth. Just because all I normally see is a tiny Birmingham portion, I must not embrace the church of God in such a parochial way. It is massive and growing and thriving, and our Lord Jesus is being proclaimed by millions of voices every second, every minute, every hour and every day. No wonder the Father delays the second coming as he waits for more and more to be saved. How wonderful it is to be a Christian in the day of the global village and at a time when stories of wonderful Christian happenings in the Spirit circulate our small yet massive world. God is *so good.*

The question we asked back on that 'Diana' Sunday – What would Jesus do? – is so pertinent to our way forward as a faith community. Jesus honoured the worship system of the synagogue and temple, yet at the same time spoke with astonishing liberty to the ordinary people. The woman at the well had put religion into her mental box, and Jesus simply broke the boundaries by his godly wisdom. We have to break those bounds, in church and society, under the guiding hand of the Spirit of God so God's church can organically flourish and people can come to faith, not in a religious system, but in the living God himself through the Lord Jesus Christ.

Of course it is clearly human nature for systems and things to become some sort of idol . . .

25

Fire from Heaven

. . . Bearing fruit in every good work, growing in the knowledge of God. (Colossians 1:10)

'Maureen, I need your help to sort out this visual aid for Sunday.' I smiled patiently at her across the vestry. My visual aids have the reputation of not working out quite as they should, so to her slightly anxious look I opinioned, 'Don't worry, this one is fine. I've got it all worked out.'

'Where have I heard that before?' she quipped back.

Maureen had 'fallen in the Spirit' in our front room some years ago[1] and was now my senior churchwarden. Not only had she grown in the faith, but so had Robert and their children. It's so good when people you have brought through to a living faith become leaders.

'Look, Maureen, you know that I'm speaking on the "pillar of fire",' I grinned. 'Well, I've got a metal bowl on the altar and I've put a few firelighters in it. Would you mind lighting them for me at the appropriate moment?'

'What do you mean, the altar? Do you mean the Lord's table?' she exasperatingly retorted. 'Anyway, you're kidding me, aren't you? I can't do that. I'll bring the whole place down.'

---

[1] See *Angels on the Walls*, p. 51.

'It won't be a problem. I've already set light to a little bit of firelighter and it was fine. It looked good and quite dramatic as well. This one won't go wrong. Believe me!'

The service was going well. All the children were really getting into the story and the moment had come to light the three or four firelighters. It was brilliant! They flared up well and illustrated the story dramatically and interestingly.

'You see,' I mouthed at Maureen crowingly.

'Now, Maureen,' I said aloud, 'please put the fire blanket over the bowl.' Turning to the children I continued patronisingly, 'And you know you mustn't play with fire, don't you?' But I realised their attention was far from me, and everybody was looking intently towards Maureen. I glanced around and saw that thick, pungent smoke was billowing from the bowl and starting to roll up the church and out amid the congregation. People staggered towards the doors and the whole service erupted into chaos!

Some may feel that such an instance is distressing, disruptive and even alienating for the worshippers. Our experience shows the exact opposite; that sharing such an outrageous occasion can be community-building. What brings down a congregation is not the extraordinary but the ordinary: the mundane ongoing week by week, month by month, year by year, almost century by century, plod. I am continually inspired and excited by Jesus' example. The folk never knew quite what to expect; witness the near sinking of the fishermen's boats, the tearing of a hole in a roof and the consequences for the pig farmers.[2]

The little prayer that Anglicans often use at the end of the psalms ('As it was in the beginning, is now, and ever shall be . . .') is a wonderful concept of the timelessness of God,

---

[2] John 21:6; Mark 2:4; Matthew 8:32.

but an alarming comment on church. The religious systems that we build up always tend to stagnate and become prosaic, whereas the living God is alive and active, and draws us towards the creative and the dramatic, even if, when we echo that theology, things occasionally go wrong.

I sat down with Maureen and the rest of my Ministry Support Team that very Sunday night and the conversation inevitably focused around the 'happening'. But after the friendly laughter had died down, it was eclipsed by another issue.

'Herbert was very disturbed this morning,' stated Maureen in her 'I'm the churchwarden' voice.

'Why was that?'

'It's that flower vase in the sanctuary. Did anyone know it was in memory of his mother? He gave it to the church about twenty-five years ago and said it was to go next to the altar! That's where it was bought for, and as far as he is concerned, that's where it will stay.'

Richard Starkie, our new churchwarden, and his wife Nicola had been asked some weeks previously to re-order the sanctuary area – brighten it up with colour and remove the inevitable clutter that had accumulated.

I reacted thoughtlessly, 'Well, I suppose we'll have to put it back. It wouldn't do to upset him. But what do you guys think?'

As a minister, I'm always conscious of an overriding need not to upset people. It's not a natural feeling for me, as I am by nature quite confrontational. I believe it is the almost sub-conscious result of clerical expectations from way back. It's somehow as if we are trained to be nice, regardless of the consequences.

'But hang on a second,' said Richard. 'How long are you going to leave it there? It's really quite inappropriate for the remodelled sanctuary. And anyway,' he pointed out with some vigour, 'if you just put it back, it will continue as some sort of idol – not just for Herbert but for his children as well. Come back in a hundred years and we'll all be gone, but the vase will still be there, even more tarnished than it is now. Get real!'

Maureen chipped in, 'Anyway, remember the roses!'

'Excuse me?'

'The roses. In the front garden of the church. In memory of . . . who was it again? They had nearly all died and made the front look really messy, but when we pulled them out, the long lost relatives emerged and were down on you like a ton of bricks! But it had to be done, didn't it?'

I remembered: 30-year-old, ill-treated, non-pruned, gnarled and faded roses. Nobody had ever claimed ownership, yet the moment we uprooted them, relatives appeared and bore down on the vicarage door in great fury. They said it was an insult to the memory of their gran. I patiently tried to explain that roses actually don't last for ever, but they were just angry. In their view, it was the church's job to maintain them for ever and ever, amen!

The church of God cannot afford to sit in the past and just be nice to everybody's memory, otherwise all our buildings will merely become historic shells rather than the living home of today's and tomorrow's church. We must not allow ourselves to be caught up in the net of everybody's expectations and whims from memories of the past, otherwise we will be hopelessly entangled in a system that is beyond our ability to change and unable to reflect the Spirit's movement for today and tomorrow. We are not here to give people what they want, but to teach them what they need in Christ. But slavery to the system would have us be nice to everybody and avoid real issues. Most of the time, however, as Herbert and the vase demonstrated, there doesn't even need to be confrontation.

What we discovered through the vase and the roses has much greater ramifications for those with historic buildings, but there is a basic truth that the church building can never be allowed to become a museum piece of past glories.

Herbert, however, became a star.

I knocked on his door with some trepidation to talk about the vase and its future.

'Come along in, Wallace,' smiled my 'problem'. I was ushered into the best room. I'd almost forgotten about the 'best room' culture of a few generations ago. The fireplace was pure 1950s, with greyish white tiles supporting an old Gasmiser fire, no doubt bought with the council's meagre offering from the Smokeless Zone Act back in the same era. The china cabinet against the flock wallpaper held the spotless, unused and unusable flowery, delicate cups with impossible handles, as well as various royal anniversary mementoes. Further into the room was the huge-sided mock leather settee, which groaned clumsily as I sank into its depths. The daintily coloured ceiling fitment, together with the lace curtains of unknown vintage, completed the picture.

Herbert happily bustled in the kitchen as I sat in his living museum and wondered what the rest of the house was like.

'Wallace, I was thinking,' he said as he re-entered, complete with tray, tea pot, biscuits and all possible accoutrements. 'I heard you were looking for somewhere to put up that student for a few months. Do you think he would like to come here? It's something I can do, you see.'

I took the proffered cup with a slightly shaky hand. 'Yes . . . that sounds good, Herbert,' I replied carefully, wondering what the bedroom might be like. Bare boards and flock mattress? Anyway, what about the vase?

We continued to talk about this and that and reminisced about his mother in an interesting and creative way, until it got past time to talk of the vase.

'Oh that,' Herbert said nonchalantly. 'It occurred to me afterwards that if we just leave it there, nothing can ever change. It will be as if we are always harking back to the olden days. Anyway, in our church, people are more important than things.'

'Yes,' I agreed between choking on biscuit crumbs.

'Wallace, what's really pressing is that new people see the Lord in our church. We mustn't worry about objects. So I've taken it away.'

'Yes,' I agreed once again. 'Now about this student . . .'

My heart was singing as I left. Not simply because my problem was solved and I also had the accommodation need sorted – albeit in a household that had never heard of duvets! I felt as if I were on cloud nine because of Herbert's spirituality. The man who had once been a totally mother-centred near recluse had become a thoughtful and proactive Christian man. He had shown me the way to deal with the vase out of a faith response.

As I arrived back at the vicarage, I swaggered in and told Mary how it was all resolved – thanks to my amazing abilities to twist people round my little finger! She soon saw through that.

'Remember how Herbert did our Christian foundations course just a few years ago?' she smiled wearily at her ego-centric spouse. 'I thought then that he was really grasping the gospel, despite years and years of being 'churched'. That's what it's all about, Wallace.'

'How do you mean?' I replied, not really wanting to know the answer.

'He's on a firm spiritual foundation. That's what I mean.

The gospel is in his heart, and his thinking has changed because of the Holy Spirit in him. It's as simple as that.'

I smiled knowingly. 'Not quite as simple, dear Mary. Just think of the effort and time in building that firm spiritual base: the teaching in church as well as your course and the house group he's joined. It's all part of a wider picture that makes Herbert who he is now.'

'OK,' she replied. 'You've got that right.' Then as an afterthought: 'For once!'

Herbert's reaction to his mother's vase may seem small fry, but there is a profound principle at work. Jesus didn't tell us merely to make converts; he told us to grow disciples. And as folk grow in that discipleship, so they are able to listen to God and discern his calling and make good spiritual decisions. It's like a Christian flow chart – and it makes sense. Herbert shows us that spiritual realities of the heart can always take us beyond the frailties of the human mind and slavery to any religious system. Because of his growing spirituality, he'd wanted to do something real for the Lord.

What so excites me about Herbert is his ability in Christ to move beyond his natural longings and needs. Instead of being a needs-based, whining Christian, he has broken through into the freedom of the Spirit. As our Lord himself said, 'If the Son sets you free, you will be free indeed.'[3]

But the devil, once one avenue is closed, always seeks another . . .

---

[3] John 8:36.

26

Adultery and Duck Ponds

> For the past troubles will be forgotten and hidden from my eyes. (Isaiah 65:16)

Religion embraces spiritual warfare. It agrees with it – in principle.

Bishops smile warily when the devil is mentioned.

Archdeacons peer over half-moon glasses and ask careful questions.

Deans make intricate notes.

New church leaders grimace encouragingly at the 'spiritual' ones, who always seem to see beyond the obvious.

Vicars preach about the Gadarene demoniac without once mentioning the demonisation of the poor man.

Church members look interested or sceptical, depending upon their developed viewpoint.

The spiritual dynamic of Satan, and he does have one, so often takes us by surprise – almost as if Paul had never said, 'Our struggle is . . . against the powers of this dark world.[1] I for one am so often lulled back into the false security of this present world that I forget the wider,

---

[1] Ephesians 6:12.

spiritual perspective. Pride comes easily to the surface and 'old forces' take control . . .

* * *

Michael, a minister from down south, rang me up. 'Wallace, are you going to that evangelical conference this time round?'

I frowned into the telephone. Not because of Michael, but because I have an irrational dislike of any conferences – necessary though I think they are. I had managed to avoid the last one of that particular genre.

'I guess,' I answered with weary interest.

'Well, I'm coming past your place, so what about if I pick you up? It'll give us a chance to have a chat as well. What do you think?'

'No problem,' I said with pleasure. 'I'd love your company.'

As Michael collected me, I noticed that he looked a bit down. His usual quite extrovert nature seemed a little dulled. But I was full of myself from a letter I'd just received.

'Michael, you'll never guess what. Kingsway have just offered to publish my book. It's called *Angels on the Walls*. I'm so amazed.'

'You've written a book?' answered my astonished friend.

'Well, actually Mary and I wrote it. Mostly Mary, really. But I do the actual pen to paper stuff, so it comes out mostly me.' I felt quite 'the man'. Had I been more sensitive, I'd have noticed that Michael seemed to shrink into the corner. But with hardly a thought I went on, 'So I've brought my laptop computer with me. I want to teach myself PowerPoint for when I get invited places. Better than sitting through all the meetings this week, don't you think?'

'PowerPoint?'

'You know – the projector display thing. Looks better than using the old-fashioned overhead.'

'Yeah, OK,' muttered my friend.

I did notice he was a bit off, but I put it down to jealousy. Oh how fallen is my nature! I went off and followed my plan and saw little of him. Of course, I hadn't listened; hadn't even acknowledged his need and concerns. But then pride is such an ear- and mind-stopper.

'Have you heard about Michael?' somebody asked a few months later. 'Did you know he's been having an affair for quite some time now and it's eventually come to a head? Just as well he has no children, otherwise it would be a mess.'

'No,' I replied with feigned innocence. Yet I had noticed something in his manner and I'd known he'd wanted to chat, but . . .'

'And did you know he's the fifth successive vicar from that particular church to get into adultery?'

No, I didn't.

Of course, it was too late. How the evil one loves to mess up the picture. Had Michael been ready to chat and work things through, or was I starting to needlessly beat myself up for being arrogant and separate? Whichever way, the devil seemed to be the winner, and the church was about to lose an excellent parish priest. However, I did note the issue about the previous four vicars. Could it be true that they had all gone down the same moral road as Michael? It hardly seemed possible.

When the new incumbent arrived at what had been Michael's church, I contacted him straight away and asked if I could call in to see him on the way down to my sister's house. It was good because Mary was with me, and she could ensure I paid attention this time.

Harry was pleased to see us. 'Come on in. You're really welcome,' he said with a huge smile. I liked him immediately. 'Come and meet Sally and we'll put the kettle on.'

Sally enthusiastically appeared as if from nowhere and happily started to show us her new home. At least some good had come out of Michael's situation,' I thought, as I observed this larger-than-life couple.

'And come and see our ducks,' Sally beamed as she led us through to the vicarage back garden. That was enough for Mary. I saw they were already friends!

I carefully explained what had happened to Michael and the four preceding vicars in their new parish: 'The last four, would you believe it? And then Michael himself. You've probably heard about that.'

They looked at each other. Obviously they had.

'Well, I must say that we're not used to this sort of thing,' admitted Harry, 'but it sounds to me as if we ought to try to do something about it.'

Sally nodded her agreement.

'Well, why don't you look up the history of this place?' Mary offered, remembering back to our Quinton Mob. 'See if what we've heard is correct and then perhaps we can get together to pray it through.'

Our little visit seemed to end at that point, and was almost forgotten about, until my email inbox showed a message from Harry: 'Like to see Mary and you about past issues. Church history relevant.'

Our quickly gathered team sat prayerfully in Harry's kitchen. Distance is really no problem when people sense there is an important spiritual job to do. Sally was there, but she soon got on with other things while Harry spoke to us.

'She really wants it all sorted out,' Harry furrowed his brow with concern, 'but she's a bit wary about anything like this, and tends to get really anxious. See what I mean?' He went on to tell us the history: 'When the church was being restored, the skeleton of a child was found somewhere underneath the old foundations – or so the story goes, although it's a bit shrouded in mystery.' Harry went on without his customary smile, 'And do you know? I've heard that some people really cursed the church because of it, but I don't know the full truth. And I haven't got a clue as to how this adultery thing fits in. But it's all a bit weird, don't you think?'

The team followed Harry to the church building and immediately started to pray. Inside the building two of our team sensed some foreboding presence. I felt totally oblivious to it, but then discernment gifts are not for all. We walked around the perimeter, scattering salt and asking for God's mercy and for cleansing of any curse that had been placed. As we came to the lychgate, Mary was given a Bible reference: 'For the past troubles will be forgotten and hidden from my eyes.'[2]

At almost the same moment, Harry said dramatically, 'I've never had anything like this before, but as Mary spoke out that verse, I had a real sense of chains overlaying the church. They were really tight – across the top and holding it down. Then just as clearly I was aware of the whole lot breaking up. Bang! They went. And the chains slithered down the sides of the building. It was really weird.' He stood and looked at us for a moment. 'Is this what normally happens?'

'If only,' I thought, thinking of the hours we often spend

---

[2] Isaiah 65:16.

in seemingly fruitless endeavour. However, Mary was getting quite hyper. 'Yes, yes. I felt something like that too. That's where the verse fits in. I'm sure of that.'

Smiles started to break out from everyone, as the reality of breaking some sort of 150-year-old curse was realised.

* * *

Harry and Sally have just completed their first four years at that church. Their ministry is excellent and I'm quite sure that the cycle of adultery has been broken. Praise God! As with our Quinton Mob and its 200 years of history, and the gallowed highwaymen of our own area,[3] it seems to me that historical events can exercise a real hold over the present. Such chains of the evil one need to be broken if we are to have an effective ministry.

Institutionalised religion agrees with such instances and gives them a churchy seal of approval, but it somehow robs them of reality. It makes them out to be little more than ecclesiastical ghost stories, attributing scant significance to them which rarely precipitates any sort of action. But how many ministries, I often wonder, have been ruined by such realities?

The system prefers things like this to be shelved as slightly extreme. It agrees with the principle, but waives practical action to avoid any confrontation. The ridiculous aspect of this attitude is that our whole faith is built on a basis of spiritual realities interpreted by God's created order. There is a real propensity for the religious establishment to patronis-

---

[3] See *Angels on the Walls*.

ingly agree with the reality of demonic forces while sidelining them with a wry smile as the 'excesses' of some evangelical Christians.

My brother or sister in Christ, we need to push and shove the dough mountain of such 'nod and wink' theology to break free of slavery to the system and get on with our business of proactive faith, even though it may well mean stirring up a hornet's nest of trouble and difficulties.

* * *

A different clergy couple rang Mary and me to help with a messy situation in their parish. I can't tell you the full details, but Moira and Guy were being victimised by a man within their congregation. He was initiating all sorts of horrible rumours. You can imagine, I guess, without me telling you. Mary and I went to see them because we knew them as a lovely, godly couple seeking to hear God.

'They were obviously distressed,' Mary remembers. 'They felt that all of their work was falling to bits around them because the congregation was being led astray by that troublemaker. And then we went into their church to pray. Wallace, don't you remember what you sensed?'

It was very spooky. As we spoke out the name of Jesus, I had a real sense of little imps coming out of the church floor and laughing at us. Scores of them. And whatever we did, more and more came.

Mary remembers, 'In the end, we just had to give up. It was a bit like the more we prayed, the greater the problem became. We were out of our depth.' It was a painful memory. 'Then, after we got back to their vicarage, Guy told us that remarkable story about the church being built near a medieval witches' ducking pool. He said it was an historical fact. And it seemed that our faith stirred up a sort of evil hornet's nest.

'Wallace,' continued my wife with her eye to the detail of the situation, 'remember how the problem with the parishioner came to a head? And Guy found it was impossible to continue, even though it was far from his fault. I don't think we helped them at all. What do you think?'

I agreed, we had failed. We were out of our depth. Or perhaps my spiritual perception was wrong. I don't know, but it was just too much, and I didn't really know of anybody I could go to for help. So we just sat on it. And what about poor Guy and Moira? Their new parish looks very promising, but how do they step over the past?

Many men and women of faith have been pole-axed by unseen spiritual forces. Many fruitful ministries have been stymied, while the religious establishment often merely pays lip-service and pragmatically avoids demonology, which may take us and them out of our depth. A church fellowship that longs to become thriving and proactive in faith needs to recognise its spiritual past. It has a 'lampstand'[4] and a spiritual identity, where Jesus is to be continually proclaimed as Lord and Saviour.

The 'old force' of pride is a shocking bedfellow. I was proud as punch to have our book published, and then along came the chance to speak at a Christian summer conference.

---

[4] Revelation 2:5.

27

Servants or Punters?

. . . but made himself nothing, taking the very nature of a servant. (Philippians 2:7)

'I see you're wearing your name badge this year,' Mary had pronounced, rather loudly in my view, earlier that morning. 'You normally look annoyed about having to wear that sort of badge, and then stick it right down on the knee of your trousers or somewhere.' She'd looked slightly amused. 'Nothing to do with the fact that it has "speaker" written on it and it's yellow instead of the normal blue, is it? Your trouble is that you fancy yourself too much,' my annoying wife had continued. 'Always wanting to be the leader, with people fawning around you.'

'Moi?' I'd questioned with faked astonishment, in a shaky French accent.

Our roadshow was a memory and even our book had become routine. I'd felt quite down until receiving the email inviting me to speak at a large Christian camp. And there I was, later that very morning, proudly sitting in the speakers' lounge feeling quite high as I rubbed shoulders with the main conference speakers – people of national renown. It made me feel important, although all I was doing was speaking at a couple of seminars along with Mary.

And I noticed, as I went round other seminars, that I'd become quite picky, inwardly critical of the speakers and counting up the numbers they had attracted. Desperately wanting to be a success, I'd even daydreamed about one of the main stage speakers becoming ill, and them asking me to fill in. Oh, the frailty of human nature and the height of original sin in our very bones!

However, I'd spoken to one of the other seminar speakers over coffee and really liked him, so I decided to go along to his seminar later that morning. Mary and I sat in the front row and I smiled at him as he started his presentation. Surprisingly, I found myself praying for him and blessing him right through the talk. And, even more amazing, the seminar blessed my socks off. Not because it was especially good, although it was, but because I went with an attitude of self-giving and prayer. I came away feeling the Lord had spoken to me in a profound way.

Mary smiled approvingly at me as we sat in our caravan eating lunch, discussing the morning. 'It reminds me of what you say about "petrol station" theology. You know – people sitting down and opening their mouths to be fed or refuelled, as if church were a "service" to them rather than to the Lord; a sort of godly petrol station.'

'OK. So what?'

'Then you remind people that Jesus said, "It is more blessed to give than to receive."[1] If they want to receive, you say, then they have to give themselves in "service" to the Lord; in worship and praise.' She smiled. 'It's as if you have been rediscovering that for yourself this morning.' Mary touched my hand lovingly. 'See what I mean, Wallace?'

It was true. On the rare occasion that I go to any meeting,

---

[1] Acts 20:35.

or anything else for that matter, with an attitude of service, I find God speaks. I can sit through the most seemingly horrific religious things with an attitude of service and be blessed. But once criticism finds its feet and I'm after things for myself, it all collapses into personal mayhem, and I merely polish the pew with my irritated backside. I become a punter.

In many churches, Christians merely go to a service rather than go to serve. Such an attitude, multiplied by the number in the congregation, leaves the meeting, whatever its denomination or type, cold and without spiritual power. It becomes just a religious service, playing the system, on yet another Sunday. And we certainly do not come to God merely to be slaves to a human system; nor do we come merely to serve ourselves. We come to worship Jesus Christ and to serve his purposes.

Mary brought this home to me later that evening as we struggled to make up the caravan beds. 'This non-serving attitude is one of the reasons why many churches see so few converts. If we all came to church with an attitude of service, it would revolutionise things overnight. What do you think?'

I think she is absolutely right. God, in his grace, so often brings the opportunities for evangelism to us, especially to our church buildings, but people who come to a church, maybe for the first time in years, needing to be met by a 'flock' who are profoundly concerned about service to God, are often met by 'punters' busy satisfying self-need.

How sure are you that both you and your fellowship bubble over with a serving attitude? Do you 'in humility consider others better than yourselves'? Is your 'attitude the same as Christ Jesus'? In your church do newcomers discover a place that is both accessible (in all senses of the word) and serving? Do they find a people whose love of Jesus overspills into a longing to serve and to demonstrate the gospel by their very attitude – 'taking the very nature of a servant'? Do they also find a fellowship alive in social action and loving concern for the needs of this world as well as the next? A Jesus society at the heart of the community?

The purpose of serving is not to give people what they want or to meet their felt needs, so allowing the church and its Lord to become some sort of doormat. Our service towards others is primarily to tell of the Saviour; that Jesus died to save us from our sins. However, it also follows that 'faith without deeds is dead', and that proclaiming Christ is not merely words but developed action towards a needy society. We must proclaim that 'Jesus Christ is Lord to the glory of God the Father' in word, action and by our very being as Christians.[2]

Never fall into the soft and unspiritual option of smiling meekly at all things regardless of truth, but ensure that all is done as a proactive, passionate and prayerful response of faith. Jesus served all people – not as they felt they needed, but in accordance with the eternal will of his Father in heaven. Do not merely change one worldly system for another and call it servanthood.

My mind immediately goes to the impact that true Christian servanthood has had on our twin fellowships of Haven and Lighthouse. One particular instance springs to mind.

I was down to lead our four gap-year young people in their regular Friday morning teaching slot. 'Culture and Faith' it was entitled. Of course, I'd forgotten all about it until I checked my diary for the following day just before going to bed. 'Oh, no! I've got no idea what to say,' I thought in panicky irreverence, but didn't say a word to Mary because

---

[2] Quotes from Philippians 2:3, 5, 7, 11; James 2:26.

she would just look at me in that way a ‘detail’ person does to the ‘untidy’. And because I’m a morning person, I knew it was no good trying to think about it through the night, so I turned over and left it in abeyance for the early morning.

After I’d taken Mary her cup of tea, I took my shower as usual and managed an arrow prayer to the Lord as the hot water cascaded. Almost immediately, my spirit responded, ‘Why don’t you just ask Mo and Jed for help?’

Mo and Jed had started coming to the Haven congregation for no apparent reason at all. They just appeared and stayed. My first real contact with Jed was when they answered a church notices advert asking if anybody wanted a free three-piece suite. He turned up at the vicarage door, looking apprehensive and slightly fearful. (It’s amazing the effect a dog collar has on some people.)

‘I’ve come about that settee . . .’ His voice trailed off.

‘Oh, the suite? No problem, Jed. You just need to pick it up from that posh new estate near the cinema – you know?’

Jed just looked at me. I cottoned on quickly to the fact that he had no means of transport or any help, and it was down to me to sort it out. He had clearly, if subconsciously, cast himself in the role of passive ‘help’, as if it were my problem.

‘This will be so bonding,’ I kidded myself as we hoisted the iron-framed settee up the narrow staircase to his maisonette. I noticed that somehow I had got the heavy end! As we accessed the third floor, a massive scurry of almost fiendish barking exploded by my left eardrum and the monstrous head of a slavering Doberman materialised about an inch from my left hand, which had become trapped against the concrete wall as I almost dropped the settee.

‘Jed,’ I shouted, with agonised hand, the settee almost in my mouth and my balance rapidly failing. ‘What’s that dog gonna do?’

Inwardly, I thought it might eat me and I pictured myself lying under the buckled settee with a broken back at the bottom of the stairs amid the accumulated muck and litter.

'It's our neighbours'. They keep it on the landing there. It's no problem.'

At that moment, an equally huge black man with amazing dreadlocks appeared behind his dog. 'What is it, man? What ya doing here?'

This was the end, I thought. Not only at the bottom of the stairs, but battered to boot.

Then he eagerly swooped down and lifted the settee with one finger, or so it seemed, and up it went into Jed's flat. I followed on in a sort of surreal slow motion, only to discover that there was already a very dirty, battered settee in situ, and little room for anything else. I looked at Jed. He looked at me. The other guy looked at us both. And Mo said, 'No problem.'

The old settee was picked up, taken to the balcony and toppled on the edge, ready to crash down the three storeys.

'Stop, stop!' I yelled, by now completely exhausted. The dog barked dramatically in the background. 'There may be some children underneath. You can't do that!'

'No problem,' announced somebody else. 'I've had a look.' And at that the settee crashed down, and I crashed down into a heap. They never prepared me for this at college!

* * *

Mo and Jed were delighted to come and chat with our four young, middle-class, gap-year people. And Mo in particular responded magnificently. She told them all about her abusive background – how she was raped at the age of 13, fell pregnant at 15, then mothered several children through different fathers, suffering all the time from a shocking lack of self-esteem and self-worth. She even told how she almost committed suicide by throwing herself off the third-floor balcony (not the same one!), and then how she had met Jed and they had started to rebuild both of their lives after feeling the inner compulsion to come along to our new Haven congregation plant.

'It's like they were all there just for me,' she said to the almost overwhelmed young people. 'Just wanting to look out for Jed and me and the kids. And it made God seem more real, so when they led the church service, we felt part of it.'

Now maybe they hit Haven on a good day, but the principle is clear. We meet, not to be mere punters and to be fed, but to serve God and others. The Holy Spirit smiles when he sees Christians intent on service. And therein rests the root of true and spirit-led evangelism. Of course we have to proclaim the gospel and do things in a prayerful and well-prepared way, but it all amounts to nothing if our worship is self-centred and our attitude is to ask, 'What's in it for me?' Slavery to any ecclesiastical system leads people to 'do' worship, as if it were complete in itself and had no inner root of spiritual reality.

At the same time, God brought John McQuay into the Haven. On the opposite end of the social scale to Jed and Mo, John is an empowered, highly able managerial accountant, even though he has personal roots on one of our estates. My then curate, Martyn Saunders, met with John to lead the funeral service of his mother, and consequently invited him to the Haven, even though John had rarely seen the inside of a church for years. What is spectacular about John is that as he came into a personal faith, he brought a servant heart. It was so easy to ask him to become the Haven churchwarden.

And there was Amy – a Kentish farm girl.

'I used to be up for the cows before 6 am,' she shared over our lunch with the free church fellowship of the northern church that allowed us a 20-minute slot in their service. 'It was when I was eleven, I remember that my older brother went out to shoot some crows. When my father and I followed him a little later, I sort of recall my brother giving the shotgun to my father. My father fiddled with it because it was broken and then suddenly it just went off. Hit my brother directly in the back of the neck. He never stood a chance. I just remember the blood and everybody shouting and the ambulance and police, and my dad crying.'

Amy took a moment to compose herself. 'It just decimated my family.' She paused and then added, 'And me. Most all of us have had nervous breakdowns since. I mean it wasn't just the gun, you see. We really weren't a happy family anyway. I remember thinking of God, but my family had never been churchgoers, so I didn't know what to do about it.'

Amy filled out her story and then ended, 'Nic and Kate Hudson invited me along to St B's – they call it Lighthouse now – and I simply knew I'd come home. It was as if God spoke to me directly as the service went on. I was just oblivious to anybody else. Do you understand what I mean?'

Amy had met with Jesus some years previously. The renewal of this embryonic and infant faith had not come through evangelism done to her. It was simply a friendly invitation from some workmates and then, as we worshipped, the Spirit of God did the rest – as he is also quietly healing her past and bringing Amy to his fullness.

There is nothing unusual here. It happens in many churches up and down the land and across the waters. But I am constantly amazed at how many people have come to faith through receiving a welcoming invitation and then, somehow, in the worship, meeting with Jesus – as if they have come home. And what powerful church members such people often make! What they sense is that God is alive and active and in the midst of the church assembly; in the midst of his serving people.

* * *

Back at the camp. Being thoroughly chastened of my pride, I went along to the thousands-strong main evening meeting resolute not to be a mere punter but filled with a sense of service: to pray for the speaker; to ask the Holy Spirit to fill the place; to ask for angels to look over us and the whole company of heaven to be upon us; to pray for the people around me and generally to bless rather than criticise. I must admit it was hard going to start with, but as the evening wore on, I discovered it was becoming a magnificent meeting with the Lord. The whole awesome experience shifted my spirituality up several notches. I had such a renewed sense of Jesus filling the whole arena and of being profoundly and personally fed by his wondrous presence. What a wonderful evening.

As we queued for ice cream afterwards (ice cream at 10.30 pm?), I related my thoughts and experience to my long-suffering wife.

'Yes, but have you thought? If you go to serve so that you can be blessed, it negates the whole thing, doesn't it? If your reason for serving is that you yourself are ministered to, then you are back where you started? Yes?' Nevertheless, she gave me a hug!

28

Pressing On

> But one thing I do: Forgetting what is behind and straining towards what is ahead, I press on towards the goal to win the prize for which God has called me heavenwards in Christ Jesus. (Philippians 3:13–14)

'Canon Brown?' The quiet voice nudged gently into my reverie. 'Canon Brown?' It was slightly louder this time and I straightened my backbone and attempted to look thoughtful and prayerful. 'Wallace, I was just going to ask your opinion on this matter. What do you think?'

Of course I had no clue what I thought, because I wasn't sure what was being talked about. But I've learned the system . . . 'Yesss. It seems an interesting thought to me, but I'd just like a little more time to give it the proper consideration.'

When I got home, I tugged out the bit of white plastic and sat down. 'Thank goodness that's over. Mary, I don't really like these meetings at all.'

'Your pride likes them though,' remarked my astute wife. 'And don't you dare forget why you're there. Remember those pictures God gave us about the moonscape and the cobweb? The canon thing isn't for your pride. It gives you an entry.'

'Yeah, yeah,' I answered with little enough grace. 'But right now all I want is a cup of tea and *The Simpsons.*' I ended with an argumentative statement rather than a question: 'Do you mind?'

*   *   *

I strongly believe that the Lord has called me into the heart of the ecclesiastical system so that I can have some sort of prophetic voice into his church – from the inside. And I was delighted several years ago when the bishop wrote to me offering the honorary title of Canon. My trouble is that I also enjoy the position and want to be recognised. But then perhaps that says more about human nature than me in particular. I also know that I am a parish priest; I still sense an excitement about community responsibility under God. Yet, I was feeling stale, slightly bored and consequently tired and irritable.

I should have seen the signs really, but people in the midst of things are often the last to know. Fortunately our break on the Isle of Lismore was only a few short weeks away. It was a chance to return to the small Scottish island I had grown to love.

With a sense of nostalgia, I entered the little and only island shop and started to hunt through their minute freezer for something to eat for tea, while Mary chatted amiably with a local resident. I didn't want people!

My hand alighted on frozen scampi. That would do. Not that there was much choice anyway, so I took it to the small counter.

'Och man, ye won't be paying that price. Get ye along to

yon strand and dig a load o' cockles. They'll be free, y'know,' said the very Scottish shopkeeper, totally ignoring the economics of his situation.

I went out without the scampi. But what did I know about cockles? I only had the vaguest idea where the strand was, having learned it was a strip of stony ground joining a very small island to the main island, but only visible at low tide for an hour at the most. 'Great!' I thought, although I had been all smiles to the shopkeeper and had thanked him profusely. 'Give me Tesco any day,' I thought unpleasantly.

Nevertheless, I thought I'd give it a go. The next day, I worked out the tides and sauntered the several miles to 'yon strand'. Of course, I got the tides all wrong and there was the water lapping gently up to create an island once again. Was all the world against me?

I tried again another day, allowing an extra couple of hours this time. And there it was: a lovely virgin strand. But where were the cockles? I suppose I expected them to be lying around like aquatic mushrooms, but they weren't. I kicked the shale and even did a bit of digging. Nothing. It occurred to me that I didn't really know what raw cockles looked like anyway.

Then it hit me. 'Wallace,' said the clear voice in my heart, 'it's time for you to move on. You've done your time at Quinton.'

Excuse me?

'I want you to move on,' said the voice. I knew it was the voice of the Holy Spirit, and I knew God had spoken about my future after nearly 18 years as Vicar of St Boniface.

'It explains it all,' I gushed at Mary later on as we ate our cockle-less snack. 'These past weeks have been quite weird and I've felt so unsettled. Not so much tired, but out of sorts with the work and myself and even the Lord. It's as if the Spirit has been preparing me. It must be.'

Mary looked both pleased and wary. 'I must say that it's time for me as well. It's my sixtieth birthday in June and I don't know if I can cope with a vicarage on the estates until you retire. But what if it goes like last time?'

I remembered back to the vicar job we'd applied for before the Bishop of Birmingham offered us St B's. There had been a massive sign on the church gable end saying 'Come and Worship the Living God' and I'd felt immensely attracted by it. At the time Mary had seen a vicarage similar to the offered one in a dream the previous night. We had returned to our church fellowship in Leicester and asked for their wisdom and prayers and a trusted intercessor had given us a word from Psalm 87:6. ('This one was born in Zion'), which we took to mean that the concept was from the Lord. We'd flung our faith at it, only to be turned down at the last hurdle when they gave the job to someone else. It was so painful. I remembered saying, 'It's all for nothing. God has no interest in me!'

However, Mary always manages to look at the faith side. 'God taught us so much through that painful experience. And it was part of the pain that led to the Lord revealing those 'angels on the walls' and how that completely changed our life and view of ministry and even of God. So it was all in his hands really. That's what that scripture means, you know, "in all things God works for the good of those who love him".'[1] She paused for a moment. 'So we'll have to go for it, won't we? I wonder how the Lord will work it out?'

* * *

[1] Romans 8:28.

Back in Birmingham following our holiday, with the experience half-forgotten, I was casually flicking through the *Church Times*. 'Team Rector @ Ipsley, Redditch' threw itself off the page at me. I sent off for the details without even telling Mary at that stage.

'Amazing,' I said to Mary a few days later, as I presented her with the unexpected paperwork. 'You know it fits us to a T. The parish has three massive estates. There is no way I could leave our prime ministry behind. But look, the mother church is in the centre of this old village. Thirteenth century. And the rectory is on the old Roman Icknield Street. You'd love that, wouldn't you?'

My application letter to the Bishop of Worcester read: 'This is my first application for many years, and I feel very excited about the Ipsley position. It seems to me to offer a new and different challenge, yet would allow me to keep an estates connection.'

A few days later, the shortlist interview details flopped onto the door mat and before I knew it I was looking round the church buildings with the interview pending. Now I knew from Lismore that God was moving me on, but I hadn't heard from him if this were the right time or place yet. I also knew that one of the questions at the interview in a few minutes would be, 'If you were offered this position, would you accept it?' What on earth should I say?

With literally a few minutes to go, I meandered towards the rector's office in the church centre. I opened the door and was totally overcome by God. I felt I had entered 'a place of peace, safety and security'.[2] Not because of its inherent beauty, but because the Lord was in this place – at least he was for me!

---

[2] Personal prophecy from Martin Thompson, 3rd August 1991.

I reflected to Mary afterwards, 'Remember how ten years ago Martin Thompson gave us a prophecy concerning moving on, and he said, "This will feel to you like Goshen"?'

'Yes, I do remember,' she replied. 'Goshen was the place where Jacob and his family settled in Egypt. By the Nile delta, if I remember rightly. A beautiful place of peace and plenty. And I recollect Martin speaking about that years ago. But fancy you remembering.'

'Well, when I entered the rector's office, I overwhelmingly heard God say, "Wallace, this is your Goshen." It was as simple as that, yet so awesome because it tied in amazingly with my encounter on Lismore. Remember? Not only that, Mary, but it was just so God. Jacob himself, after that wonderful encounter with God and all the angels on the stairway at Bethel, later on settled in Goshen. So I knew this was it, and I told the panel as well. I wonder what they thought?'

A very short time afterwards, the bishop rang and offered me the post. I knew he would, and I immediately accepted.

God is so amazing. The move nearly 18 years before had been torture. I went through the most horrific personal and spiritual trauma. Clearly, as I look back, it was God's hand and his way of teaching me for the future, but it was not so clear at the time – 'caustically devastating' would be a better phrase. This time it flowed in a matter of a few weeks. All the ends fitted together and it was just very God. Yet both must have been very God. It's just that my eyes, mind and humanness prefer the latter way!

When you seek God's pathway through your life, do you automatically expect the Lord to smooth it, making it easy and painless? Do you simply trust the system to work it out and bring forth a godly result? Indeed, do you use good old common sense or your intellectual prowess, with God on the back burner, expected to come up with the goods? It seems to me that the Christian world is far too full of casualties who have, quite wrongly, expected God to 'magic' a way forward for them and then wonder why it all comes apart at the seams. How easy to blame God at that point and become a secretly sceptical 'renewed' Christian!

As I read of our Lord and all the apostles, as well as Christians down the ages, I clearly see God working out his plan and purposes. Yet for them and us, ease or difficulty is no test at all. 'God just opened doors' is not a scriptural imperative. There is a truth within that statement, but it's not as straightforward as a clear road on an open landscape. What sets 'calling' apart, be it job, ministry or lifestyle, is a spiritual attitude of proactive dynamic faith expressing that God is totally involved – whatever – and will ultimately have his way, providing that we make him number one, to the best of our prayerful ability.

Some months later, Mary and I sat in a hotel in Liverpool at a Christian leaders' conference. At our small breakfast table, we were joined by two other Christian couples.

'Good morning. Good conference, do you think?' I opened the conversation.

They offered the standard replies and we got to talking about what they did, because vicars get very good at cross-questioning people.

The older couple replied, 'Well, we're retired now, so we have time to come to conferences like this. And afterwards we're off in our caravan.'

I was quite surprised. 'Do you mind me asking how old you are?'

'Not at all. Cedric is just turning fifty-seven this year, aren't you dear?'

At this the wife of the younger couple sprang to life. 'Oh,

we're retired as well. Great, isn't it! You can do just what you like.' She didn't sound very convincing.

'Well, I have to tell you,' I said, 'I've just got a new job, with a bigger parish and team vicars and everything, and I'm fifty-nine this year.'

Silence reigned. I'd discovered how to stop conversation!

But the truth is, as Christians we never retire. Can you imagine St Paul saying, 'Sorry, I can't come and speak. I'm retired now'? It may be that we give up our day job and retire in the world's eyes, but we remain warriors for the kingdom as long as we have breath in our body. Some of the best teaching I've ever received has emanated from the lifestyle of much older Christians who are living on the fringe of death with Jesus at the centre of their lives. These two couples had opted out, or so it seemed, and were enjoying the 'entertainment' value of the conference and the little work they did in their 'Middle England' home churches.

The system of this world can so often lead to the ageism that closes us down. Many active and able older Christians who ought to be able to exercise faith without the often lifelong boundaries of job and children are caught in the trap of a nostalgic 'my day', which mitigates against active involvement in the battlefield of this generation.

Are you clear that Jesus has a job for you to do, a role for you to get involved in, till the day you die? I am certainly much slower now, and need time to sort myself out and greater leisure to destroy tiredness, but you and I are soldiers of the kingdom of God, and there is much work to be done, whether you are seven or seventy. But the system will so often shackle, and the devil will smile – as well he might.

God wants all Christians to be his soldiers. Not in any

bloodthirsty sense, but as his people standing up, in faith, for the wonderful gospel imperative. There are no age, colour or sex limitations on God's wonderful calling to all people to proclaim Jesus Christ as Lord.

* * *

'Wallace, I've read your story about me – about the prison cell and Saffron and all that,' Gaynor told me. 'That was right and it brought tears to my eyes to remember it. But you implied later on that Jackson's coming home would tear Saffron away from the Lord, and I know that I also went through a testing time with all the emotions it stirred up in me. But I want to tell you that you were wrong. They are an item now, and although he's nowhere near being a Christian, as far as I know, he respects her. Saffron is still following Jesus and they are getting married. Good, isn't it?'

Gaynor herself has gained her qualifications as an accredited Christian counsellor. She has her own calling card and later this year she will have her secular counselling diploma. I have sent quite a few people to her for counselling and she is brilliant. As she would say, 'I've been there, and bought the tee shirt.'

The system would try to marginalise the Gaynors of this world, first by erecting unseen yet unsurmountable barriers – hurdles for them to jump over, often knowing that they will fall – and secondly by seeking to turn them into middle-class people so they lose all sense of their roots. Our Jesus loves Gaynor and wants her to express her wonderful faith with wide eyes and authentic background, and our job is to buck the system to open up pathways for the

Gaynors of this world. The church of God is not about religion, but about God in love with people and people in love with God.

Mary and I don't know where the future lies. At Redditch, for a season I'm sure, but beyond that, who knows? But one thing is certain: with God our future, on this earth or the next, is totally assured. He is in control and he is Lord and Saviour. When our lives are in his hands, 'all is well and all manner of things are well'.[3]

[3] Mother Julian of Norwich.

Angels on the Walls

by Wallace and Mary Brown

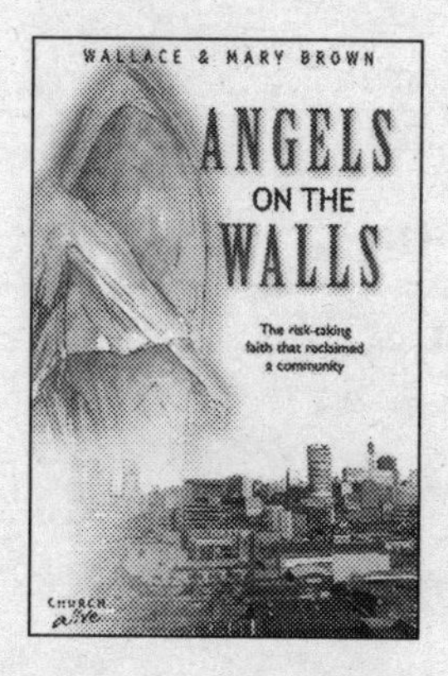

What happens when a church situated in the middle of a Birmingham housing estate dares to lower its protective barricades against the violence and crime all around, and invite the hooligans to come inside? The result is risk-taking faith that reclaims a community for Christ and goes on to reach out to a whole nation.

This moving and astonishing true story by Wallace Brown and his wife, Mary, will inspire churches of all denominations.